CAMP BLANDING
FLORIDA STAR IN PEACE AND WAR

Camp Blanding
Florida Star In Peace and War

W. Stanford Smith

RTP
RESEARCH TRIANGLE PUBLISHING

Published by
Research Triangle Publishing, Inc.
Fuquay-Varina, NC 27526

ISBN 1-884570-80-1

Library of Congress Catalog Card Number: 97-76543

Cover Design by Kathy Holbrook

Photographs and maps reproduced by permission of Camp Blanding
Museum and Historical Associates.

∞The paper used in this publication meets the minimum requirements of the
American National Standard for Information Sciences—Permanence of Paper
for Printed Library Materials, ANSI Z39,48-1984.

Printed in the United States of America
10 9 8 7 6 5 4 3 2 1

The Minuteman is the symbol of the citizen soldier, a universal term which includes the National Guard and all the other Reserve Components of all the services, all ranks, both sexes and all who have responded to the call to the colors in every conflict in which this nation has been involved.

Citizen soldiers made up the preponderance of all units and organizations serving at Camp Blanding throughout its history recounted in this book.

Major General Blanding,
for whom Camp Blanding was named.

TABLE OF CONTENTS

APPRECIATION

The idea for this book originated with Lt. Col. Norman L. Redding, full-time training site manager and deputy post commander of Camp Blanding in 1996. He has collaborated with the author throughout the many months of research. His wife Mary and my wife Martha have been much more than supporting spouses. As active participants, they helped with interviews, suggested more sources, critiqued writings and provided continuous encouragement.

Special mention must be accorded Rodney P. Hall, the first director of the Camp Blanding Museum and now president of Camp Blanding Museum and Historical Associates. He guided the author to a majority of the sources of the World War II section of the book and shared his many years of personal experience at Blanding. James F. Bloodworth, first president of the Museum Associates, provided significant information and suggestions which enhanced the validity of the author's research.

Leon S. Theil, Camp Blanding public relations officer 1943-1945, provided both documentation and personal remembrances, then reviewed the manuscript for the author. Harry M. Hatcher, a former post commander, likewise provided personal recollections and a review of the manuscript.

This page could not list all the others who provided major help to the author. Their names appear in the Sources section of the book.

Aerial view of Camp Blanding as early as February 1941.

INTRODUCTION

Camp Blanding's history is a tale of superb accomplishment by many thousands of individuals over more than half a century. Its glory days began two years before U.S. entry into World War II when its heavily wooded, mostly sandy, partly swampy terrain was transformed into a training site for the Florida National Guard. Camp Blanding was expanded in size and given additional missions when war came with the result that it played a major role in successful prosecution of that war. It provided training for nine U.S. Army divisions, it was the activation site for the famous 508th Parachute Infantry regiment and dozens of other separate units, it provided training for many thousands of individuals through an Infantry Replacement Training Center after the divisions left for combat and for some Allied troops under special arrangements. It was the home also of a major hospital, a prisoner of war camp, a large reception center and finally a separation center when the war came to an end.

Throughout its history Camp Blanding is a success story. The State Armory Board and a succession of Florida Adjutants General exercised leadership that made possible the achievements of World War II and the many innovations of the post-war Florida National Guard continuing today.

Thousands of Floridians contributed to the success story that is Camp Blanding. The nearest city is Starke in Bradford County. It became a boom town when the camp was constructed in 1939—1941. The civilian population responded to the needs of the expanded military installation with patriotic fervor. Located in Clay County, the camp is oriented toward both Starke and the town of Green Cove Springs in Clay County which also gave its full support to the Army and to Camp Blanding. Both of those cities had military installations or units in World War II

Located forty miles southwest of Jacksonville and west of St. Augustine, Camp Blanding today is a 72,000 acre training site owned and operated by the state of Florida for the Florida National Guard. It is frequently used also by National Guard troops of other states and by the active and reserve component armed forces of the United States and other nations. It also serves the public interest in wildlife management and environmental protection as well as recreation facilities for hunting and fishing.

The good judgment of the state of Florida in taking ownership and developing Camp Blanding over the past fifty years is demonstrated every day. This book tells the story of Camp Blanding through its entire history as seen by those who experienced that history in the 20th century.

EARLY HISTORY

Even before Camp Blanding was conceived, this land had a long and turbulent history with many battles involving Indians, Spanish, French, English, American union troops and Confederates. The land was watered with blood in battles as early as the sixteenth century and was involved in various ways in subsequent conflicts in the eighteenth, nineteenth and twentieth centuries.

Camp Blanding is located in the first part of the Florida peninsula. Although the highest elevation in the area is only about 250 feet, it is referred to in Florida as the central highlands because it rose above sea level during the Pleistocene Era. Astride a geological formation known as Trail Ridge is an ore body containing heavy, mineral sands that are being mined by the DuPont Company under contract with the state of Florida. The terrain of the entire area offers such variation in natural growth that it is suitable for almost all types of military training.

Wildlife has always been plentiful in the area, which now includes a Wildlife Management Area within the boundaries of Camp Blanding where threatened species are protected.

Hunting is allowed in season under controlled conditions in certain areas of Camp Blanding.

Major geographical features are Kingsley Lake, Varnes Lake, Whitamore Lake, Stevens Lake, Blue Pond, Lowry Lake, Magnolia Lake, Black Creek and Trail Ridge. Camp Blanding abuts about half the shoreline of Kingsley Lake. The lake is almost perfectly round, about two miles in diameter, and believed by most geologists to have been formed from a giant sinkhole. The depth is about ninety feet at its deepest point. It is fed by underground springs, and its cool pure water feeds the South Prong of Black Creek. The Florida Department of Environmental Regulation on petition protects these waters as "Outstanding Florida Waters" designated as such in 1990 by residents of the area, local governments and the Florida National Guard.

Trail Ridge runs from what is now the Georgia state line into this area. The Alachua Trail, which follows this ridgeline, provided a favorite route for Indians and later for settlers. Several Indian tribes used Trail Ridge and the St. Johns River/ Black Creek waterway as far back as 5,000 B.C. to enter the western portion of Clay County which later became known as Camp Blanding.

The wide and deep St. Johns River attracted European settlers just as it had provided sites for Indian settlements along its banks. It is about twenty miles east of Camp Blanding but a major tributary Black Creek flows through part of Camp Blanding. Indians called the river Weelaka, the French named it *Riviere de Mai*, the Spanish called it *Rio de San Juan*, and the English gave it the name St. Johns. The river retained the name St. Johns due to English influence. It is one of the few rivers in the world that flows south to north.

The earliest Indian tribe known to inhabit the area were the Timucua, a generally peaceful group first encountered by the French explorer Jean Ribault in 1562. The Spanish regarded this as an intrusion into their colonial territory. A Spanish force defeated the French in 1565, slaughtered the French settlers and moved on to develop St. Augustine, the oldest city in the United States.

Today St. Augustine enjoys a close relationship to Camp Blanding. The Florida National Guard Headquarters, of which Camp Blanding is a subordinate command, is located in the historic St. Francis Barracks now known as the State Arsenal in St. Augustine. The history of the State Arsenal parallels in many ways that of the lands that became Camp Blanding. Originally the British converted a Spanish Franciscan monastery building to a military reservation when Spain in the Treaty of 1763 ceded Florida to England. Like Camp Blanding, the State Arsenal today is owned and operated by the state of Florida. Spain was the dominant force in Florida in the late sixteenth century. The Spanish established missions to bring Christianity to the Indians but drew their enmity by conscripting them for forced labor.

The English established a settlement at Charleston, South Carolina, in 1670, thus presenting a new threat to the Spanish. Intermittent fighting ensued between the English and Spanish with the French also involved from 1745 until 1748 when the English defeated them. The Spanish were also defeated by the English and were ousted from North America by the Treaty of Paris in 1763. By this date also inter-tribal rivalry had left the Seminoles as the dominant Indians in Eastern Florida but the Creeks were still present in the area that became Camp Blanding. By treaty in 1765 the Creeks ceded to the British certain lands in the eastern part of what became Clay County, keeping for themselves the area now occupied by Camp Blanding. However, action by the British government in London encouraged settlements in Florida through grants to families settling in the area, including a large plantation on the Black Creek to the Colville family.

The American Revolution, 1775—1783, resulted in some conflicts in the area between Loyalists and American colonists. The Treaty of Paris in 1783 recognized American independence but Florida was ceded back to Spain.

Zephaniah Kingsley, a wealthy Scottish slave trader, entered the area in 1803. He was able to import slaves for a cost of about fifty dollars each and sell them for about $1,000 each to plantation owners in north Florida, Georgia and South Carolina. It seems likely that Kingsley Lake derived its name from this Kingsley or one of his progeny. Legend has it that the lake was named for a cavalry officer, a Captain Kingsley who became surrounded by Indians on a trail south of the lake and had to swim his horse across the lake to escape capture. It is said the horse died of this exertion. If this event actually occurred, it seems likely Captain Kingsley was a relative of Zephaniah.

The second occupation of Florida by the Spanish was marked by continued conflicts with Indians and migrating Americans who wanted Florida to become part of the United States. This finally came about after the War of 1812 by treaty between the United States and Spain on February 22, 1821. Many Spanish departed and many Americans migrated to this area of Florida, attracted by the climate and recreational facilities as well as the opportunities for business. For the same reasons Clay County continues to increase in population today.

The American Civil War (still referred to in the South as the War Between the States) brought turmoil to the area. As Union and Confederate forces fought in north Florida in 1864, it is likely that some contact took place in the area now occupied by Camp Blanding. Arriving from South Carolina at the mouth of the St. Johns River on Feb. 7, 1864, Union forces advanced across north Florida generally along the route of the Florida, Atlantic and Gulf Central Railroad but on a broad front. The main battle took place at Olustee near Lake City. Consolidating their positions at various points along the way, Union forces sent expeditions south to Gainesville, Middleburg and Starke. Patrols going to Starke would have inevitably come within the confines of the present Camp Blanding. After the war and reconstruction, population growth continued and the area became popular, attracting many prominent people as visitors and as residents.

Farming and lumbering sustained the permanent residents in the late years of the nineteenth century. Oranges, strawberries and grapes were grown. However, in 1895 a "big freeze" sent temperatures down to a low of eight to ten degrees. This brought the end of successful citrus farming in this part of Florida.

The city of Starke, which experienced explosive growth when Camp Blanding was established, entered the picture in the immediate area when Comer L. Peek, a Starke real estate man, developed land on the west side of Kingsley Lake. Peek sold sixty-foot lots for fifty dollars to many residents of Starke for summer cottages. Roads from Starke were eventually improved. Many families built modern homes on the lake and became permanent residents. Many others used these homes to escape the sizzling summer heat. This was the nature of the area of Camp Blanding until the years just before World War II.

When Camp Blanding was built (1939-1941), this was the office of the constructing Quartermaster.

THE MILITIA COMES OF AGE

From the time of the first settlers in Florida, volunteers formed organized military forces to meet the needs of the times. They were known variously as Florida Rangers, State Militia or Florida State Troops.

Soon after the treaty was ratified making Florida a territory of the United States in 1821, Congress placed the new territory directly under the president. General Andrew Jackson was made governor of Florida. The whole territory was not under firm control because of pirates and smugglers in the coastal towns, runaway slaves and uncontrolled Seminole Indians in the interior.

The need for a militia was apparent, and volunteers responded. Records show that 29,953 volunteers were employed in the Seminole Wars of 1835—1843 along with 10,169 regulars. The uniforms of the militia of that time were anything but uniform. It appeared that no two soldiers were dressed alike. They carried whatever weapons they could lay hands on and rode horses of all sizes and kinds.

The Legislature soon took action to improve the status of the militia. It authorized the governor to appoint officers and appropriated funds to pay them, even enacting laws to protect the property rights of militiamen while they served on active duty, much as National Guard and other reserve component members are protected by federal laws today.

When Florida became a state in 1845, one of the first acts of the new Legislature was titled "An Act to Organize the Militia of the State of Florida." That act made virtually all able bodied white males liable for militia duty and provided for uniforms and equipment for the troops. These militia forces were employed extensively against the Indians, so much so that only two companies of volunteers from Florida were sent to Mexico in the Mexican War.

The American Civil War was another story. Florida seceded from the Union January 3, 1861, and became a major supplier and the storehouse of the Confederacy. Beef and vegetables were produced in the state; medicines and other supplies came from sympathetic blockade-runners through the Bahamas. Most of the battles were fought elsewhere, but whatever engagements took place in Florida, the militia was the defending force.

Under the harsh terms of reconstruction and federal military rule, Florida's militia was forced into a period of inactivity. After about eight years, Florida regained control of its own fate, and the militia was reorganized. By 1893, the Florida State Troops were reported to include twenty companies of infantry and two batteries of light artillery. It remained this size until the Spanish-American War. President McKinley called for volunteers, asking Florida to supply one regiment of infantry from the State Militia. All of the Florida companies volunteered. The first unit to volunteer was said to be the Starke unit known locally as Company B, Fourth Separate Battalion. The volunteer companies were consolidated into the required regiment of twelve companies. The Starke unit became Company M of the 1st Florida Volunteer Regiment. Fearing attacks by the Spanish on the coasts, Florida residents organized new units to provide for coastal defense and a naval militia was likewise organized.

After the Spanish-American War, the militia was again reorganized. The first call to what is now known as state active duty came soon when troops were ordered to Jacksonville in 1901 to preserve order at the great Jacksonville fire. This mission was a success but jealousies and controversies among units led to an important development; namely, the plan for an annual encampment of all Florida militia units. Such a plan was not immediately implemented but the need for such training led ultimately to the establishment of Camp Blanding (and its predecessor Camp Foster).

The term National Guard came into use about this time, and in 1903 the National Guard Association was formed. To this day that organization plays a major role in promoting the professionalism, budgetary support and public relations of the National Guard at the national and state level. The Florida State Troops officially became the Florida National Guard in 1909 when the Legislature enacted a new military code.

In 1916 the Second Florida Infantry regiment of the Florida National Guard, commanded by then Colonel Albert H. Blanding, was mobilized for duty on the Mexican border chasing Pancho Villa. The regiment returned home for release from active duty in April 1917. Because of its outstanding service on the Mexican Border, this regiment was designated the 124th Infantry in September 1917 upon mobilization for World War I along with other units of the Florida National Guard. The 1st Florida Infantry was split among units of the 31st "Dixie Division." A total of 42,030 Floridians served on active duty in World War I, of whom 1,287 were killed in action or died in service.

After the end of World War I, the United States neglected its military at all levels. On January 1, 1919, Florida had no federally recognized National Guard. During that year the Militia Bureau of the War Department issued new regulations for reorganization of the National Guard. Lack of public support and reluctance of young men to join led to slow progress. In 1920 the Florida National Guard strength was only 836 officers and enlisted men. Public support increased later in the decade and strength gradually increased. These troops were urgently needed in September 1926 when a hurricane devastated Dade County. All units in the Miami, Fort Lauderdale and Hollywood area were called to duty. They served effectively to preserve order and protect property, much as the Florida National Guard has done in recent years on the occasion of several devastating hurricanes.

Brigadier General J. Clifford R. Foster served as Adjutant General of Florida 1901—1916 and 1923—1928. He died in 1928 and was succeeded by Brigadier General Vivian Collins who continued to serve throughout World War II when the Florida National Guard established another distinguished record.

CAMP FOSTER:
CAMP BLANDING PREDECESSOR

The urgent need for a training site suitable for annual encampments of all Florida National Guard units was noted as early as 1901 when units had difficulty working together on active duty at the great Jacksonville fire. The Florida Legislature in 1905 responded to this need by appointing a commission to examine potential areas and recommend a suitable site large enough to accommodate campgrounds and a rifle range. The commission visited and inspected a large number of sites, finally recommending a location known as Black Point near Yukon in Duval County.

This site was deemed suitable because of its healthful climate, general physical characteristics and proximity to transportation. It was eight miles from Jacksonville by paved road. The original tract was only 300 acres but additional land nearby was available which could be acquired for a rifle range adjacent to the campgrounds. The War Department approved purchase of this additional land from funds appropriated for equipment and support of the National Guard and the promotion of rifle practice.

The federal government then purchased a tract of 400 acres August 10, 1907, two tracts of eighty-five acres and $108\frac{1}{3}$ acres on September 11, 1908, and 100 acres on November 18, 1913. The total area of federal and state land was then $993\frac{1}{3}$ acres.

This made quite a satisfactory training site with many characteristics similar to those of Camp Blanding today. It was an attractive area heavily wooded with magnolia and oak trees and sandy soil with natural drainage on a peninsula from the west shore of the St. Johns River. Water was supplied from a ten-inch artesian well with an estimated flow of 2,500,000 gallons per day.

Camp facilities were constructed of sufficient size to accommodate a brigade of infantry who at that time consisted of two regiments. These facilities included kitchens and latrines, administration building, officers club, warehouses, caretaker quarters, swimming pool, post exchange building and dance pavilion.

The principal training facility was the rifle range constructed to specifications of the National Board for the Promotion of Rifle Practice, an agency of the War Department. It had rifle firing points to ranges as long as 1,000 yards and also facilities for pistol and machine gun firing.

Originally named Camp Joseph E. Johnson for a Confederate general from Florida, the camp was used extensively for training in World War I. In 1929 it was redesignated Camp Foster in honor of Brigadier General J. Clifford R. Foster, the Adjutant General of Florida, who had died the year before.

In the years between the two world wars Camp Foster served as the field-training site not only for the Florida National Guard but also for troops of other southeastern states. In like manner, Camp Blanding today serves as training site for active and reserve units and sometimes for foreign troops in addition to the Florida National Guard. It was jointly owned by the state of Florida through the State Armory Board and by the federal government through the War Department.

The Florida State Armory Board was created by the state legislature in 1921 and given broad statutory authority to manage and control "all military buildings and real property within the state applied to military uses." The statute provides that the Armory Board consists of "the Governor, the Adjutant General, the Assistant Adjutants General, the State Quartermaster, and commanders reporting directly to the Adjutant General, in the active National Guard of the state." The governor is the chairman, and the Adjutant General is vice-chairman.

This enactment obviated the necessity to create a commission, as was done in the acquisition of Camp Foster. The Armory Board played a major role, as it does today, at every step in the acquisition of land, development and operation of Camp Blanding.

The statute (Chapter 250.40 and 250.41) gave the Armory Board specific authority to accept land or buildings contributed by local governments and also to exercise the right of eminent domain to seize property needed for military uses and compensate the owners through the courts. This authority was used extensively in acquisition of land for Camp Blanding.

Today the Armory Board meets quarterly and continues to exercise authority over land acquisition, construction and use of armories and other buildings for military purposes. Camp Foster effectively met the needs of the Florida National Guard during the ensuing years until what turned out to be a fortuitous circumstance developed in 1939. The United States Navy expressed a desire to acquire both the land owned by the state and the federal land to establish a Naval Air station. This met with enthusiastic response within the Jacksonville Chamber of Commerce and the local county and city governments. The Duval County Air Base Authority was organized to purchase the necessary property for this installation. A sequence of events then resulted in transfer of the land to the navy for its Naval Air station and soon thereafter led to the purchase of land to establish what became Camp Blanding.

The year was 1939, and war had already erupted in Europe even as the Japanese were flexing their muscle throughout the western Pacific. National defense became a serious concern in the United States. The Florida Legislature in May directed the State Armory Board to convey to the Duval County Air Base Authority, for use by the United States Navy, all state owned lands within Camp Foster.

Various conditions were placed on these transactions by the parties involved, resulting in heavy administrative and legal burdens on the Adjutant General, the State Armory Board and the governor. First, the War Department would not agree to release its part of Camp Foster to the navy unless the Florida State Armory Board was compensated in the amount of $400,000 plus salvage rights for its property at Camp Foster. The War Department also required that before relinquishing the property, it be assured that a suitable camp and facilities would, in fact, be established elsewhere in Florida at no cost to the War Department over and above normal allotments to the Florida National Guard and that the new site be leased to the federal government without cost.

There was another problem in disposing of Camp Foster and building a new camp. The deed, which transferred to the state title to the Camp Foster property, contained a clause that nullified the title in the event the site was abandoned by the National Guard. To sell the property to the Duval County

Air Base Authority, it was necessary to get a quit claim deed from the Jacksonville Chamber of Commerce. Even though the Naval Air station was much desired by Jacksonville and Duval County, the chamber declined to release its claim on the grounds that the original transfer was made solely with the view of obtaining the commercial benefits a military camp might bring to the community. To solve this problem the State Armory Board entered into an agreement with the Jacksonville Chamber of Commerce to the effect that a new site would be purchased as close to Jacksonville as could be found which met the requirements of the Armory Board and the approval of the War Department.

The Air Base Authority was authorized by the state of Florida to issue and sell bonds in the amount of $1,100,000 of which $400,000 was to be transferred to the State Armory Board for the purpose of establishing and equipping a suitable National Guard camp elsewhere.

The contract between the State Armory Board and the War Department was executed September 11, 1939. Vivian Collins, Adjutant General of Florida, signed for the Armory Board, and Harry H. Woodring, Secretary of War, signed for the federal government. The implementing clause of that contract follows:

> NOW, THEREFORE, it is mutually agreed by and between the parties hereto:
>
> 1. The funds paid by the Board of Commissioners of the Duval Air Base Authority to the State Armory Board of the state of Florida in the amount of four hundred thousand dollars ($400,000.00) will be expended by said Board for the acquisition of land and construction of necessary facilities for the re-establishment of the present National Guard Camp in a suitable

location elsewhere, provided that not to exceed $100,000.00 of the above sum shall be expended for the acquisition of not less than approximately 25,000 acres of land, and provided further that the new camp site and maneuver area will be leased to the United States without cost to the federal government for a period of ninety-nine (99) years, and provided further that no land will be acquired or facilities installed or constructed with any part of the aforesaid $400,000.00 without prior approval of the Secretary of War; and, it is further agreed that essential facilities adequate to accommodate one Regiment of Infantry will be completed by July 1, 1940. Provided further that nothing in this agreement will prevent the expenditure of reasonable sums for administrative purpose incident to the acquisition of land and the construction of facilities thereon.

2. That upon the execution of this agreement, the Secretary of War will transfer to the jurisdiction of the Navy Department the existing Black Point Military Reservation consisting of approximately six hundred and eighty-two (682) acres of land.

3. The performance of this agreement is contingent upon obtaining such Congressional authority thereof as may be necessary."

The check from the Duval County Air Base Authority in the amount of $400,000 was received November 18, 1939, and deposited with the state treasurer to the credit of the "Armory Board Replacement Fund."

The new camp site turned out to be the Kingsley Lake area acquired after another series of complications and given the name Camp Blanding in honor of Major General Albert H. Blanding, a Floridian who served in the War Department as Chief of the National Guard Bureau.

It should be noted here that as early as 1935, an increased level of combat training of the Florida National Guard called for more expansive maneuver area than was available in the Camp Foster vicinity. As General Collins explained in 1941 to the War Department, "to meet this situation, the troops encamped at Camp Foster found and utilized the present Camp Blanding area for field exercises to the entire satisfaction of all commanders and to federal instructors and inspectors."

Company formation before the company street of World War II hutments.

BUYING THE LAND

Selecting the site and acquiring the land for the new camp turned out to have as many problems and complications as the sale of Camp Foster. Faced with the urgency of the project, the State Armory Board had to satisfy conditions laid down in the contract by the War Department and in the agreement with the Jacksonville Chamber of Commerce while meeting the needs of the Florida National Guard and gaining approval of Governor Fred P. Cone who was active in this endeavor throughout the process.

As noted above, the expanded combat training of the National Guard required much larger areas. In fact, the new camp was to be more than twenty-five times as large as Camp Foster. To meet this requirement, the Armory Board investigated six potential sites—the Talquin area in Gadsen County, the Eastport area in Duval County, the Dinsmore area in Duval County, the DeLand area in Volusia County, the Green Cove Springs area in Clay County and the Kingsley Lake area in Clay County.

The Armory Board adopted the following criteria for the selection process:

1. Health (water, drainage, mosquitoes)
2. Accessibility to units of Florida National Guard
3. Rail and highway facilities
4. Cost of property
5. Range for artillery firing
6. Availability of adjoining lands for field maneuvers
7. Access to markets for food supplies
8. Recreation (swimming, boating, fishing)

On September 10, 1939 (one day before the contract between the War Department and the Armory Board was signed), the War Department sent a Board of Regular Army experts into the state to assist the Armory Board in reaching a decision on the new camp site.

All proposed sites in Duval County were eliminated because they did not have adequate area for infantry and artillery training and because their prices were too high. The Kingsley Lake area was selected because it came closest to meeting the eight criteria above and it also met the requirement of being as close to Jacksonville as could be found meeting necessary requirements including War Department approval.

The Kingsley Lake site received favorable coverage in the Jacksonville newspapers. Headlined "Only 27 Miles Away," an article in the *Jacksonville Journal* displayed a map of the proposed camp and pointed out that "the Armory Board kept it inside the Jacksonville trade area just as it promised to do." The article anticipated 5,000 men training at the new camp would have "nowhere else to go" but to Jacksonville in their time off.

Explaining and justifying the site selection in a letter to the War Department May 16, 1941, General Collins wrote:

> The Armory Board is convinced that its selection was sound and that the lands comprising Camp Blanding and its location was the best

available within the state. It is pointed out that this tract is located on the watershed of the peninsula. The elevation of Kingsley Lake is 176 feet and its waters drain to the east while one mile west of the lake, surface water drains to the west. No other place found within the state was so free of mosquitoes. The waters of the seven lakes within the area are among the purest and clearest within the state. The rolling sand hills within the artillery area furnishes an outstanding range for heavy weapons.

The War Department requested this explanation to respond to inquiries by the Senate Investigating Committee headed by Sen. Harry S. Truman. This response apparently satisfied Senator Truman. His work as head of this committee checking out defense administration during the war helped make Senator Truman a plausible nominee for vice president and ultimately president of the United States.

Consummation of the land purchases lagged behind work on the camp itself but it was clear to all that the required land would be acquired by the state and federal governments. At issue was the price to be paid to the numerous owners.

To expedite these urgent transactions, Florida Attorney General J. Tom Watson retained Attorney Richard P. Daniel of Jacksonville to assist the Adjutant General and the Armory Board in resolving the many legal issues, particularly land acquisition. This legal work turned out to be quite extensive and involved many details in the acquisition of many separate tracts of land in 1939, 1940 and 1941.

Summarizing this work in a letter to the state attorney general May 30, 1941 (when much of this work was still going on) attorney Daniel wrote:

We rendered opinions on the titles to these lands, based upon numerous abstracts of title, with varying terminal dates. ...We directed the appraisal of these lands by the Board's Appraisers J. Alvin Register and Walter D. Shelly. We conducted negotiations with various claimants of ownership of portions of said lands, and where marketable titles were offered at not exceeding appraisedprices, we closed purchases by the Board. Where claimants were willing to accept not exceeding appraised values, but had defective, though curable, titles, we obtained execution of curative instruments where possible; and where impossible, we filed suit and obtained decrees quieting title.

Where owners have refused to sell at not exceeding appraised values, or had incurable defective titles, we filed a Petition for Condemnation of such lands in the Circuit Court for Clay County, Florida, naming the Armory Board as Plaintiff, against all persons shown by the abstracts to have any claims whatever. We prosecuted this suit to completion and attended to payment into Court by the Board of the awards made by the Final Judgment, and attended to distribution thereof as ordered.

Still more legal work was involved in the execution of leases to the War Department and in the acquisition of additional land authorized and funded by action of the state legislature in 1941. Attorney Daniel did this work for the Armory Board as it would have been impossible for the full-time staff of the National Guard or even of the Attorney General's Office to perform so many details.

The initial purchases by the state were for 28,200 acres from Foremost Properties, Inc., in six transactions between December 28, 1939 and November 25, 1941. These purchases are recorded in public records of Clay County in Deed Book 38, page 157; Deed Book 38, page 301; Deed Book 38, page 376; Deed Book 39, page 34; Deed Book 39, page 448, and Deed Book 41, page 222. The 1941 appropriation of $21,240 was used to purchase an additional 2,840 acres, bringing state ownership up to 31,040 acres.

The contract between the Armory Board and the War Department provided that this land would be leased to the United States without cost to the federal government. When the United States entered World War II December 7, 1941, it became apparent that much more land would be needed to provide training for the size units contemplated for the new camp. Accordingly, the War Department entered upon a program to acquire these additional lands through Eminent Domain proceedings in United States District Court in Jacksonville. The result was eight separate judgments by the Court referred to as Takings No. 1, 2, 3, 4, 5, 6, 7 and 8, recorded in the public records of Clay County from December 14, 1942 to March 31, 1943.

Commenting on the history of these land acquisitions, Clay County Attorney William D. Moore wrote in a letter to the Camp Blanding commander May 3, 1984, that "According to local tradition, the United States Government taking was done in some haste, responding to War Department requirements. In some instances, landowners had barely time to round-up their cattle, then permitted under Florida law to range at large, before government contractors appeared to clear and burn trees located on the site for construction of barracks."

Because of the urgency of these acquisitions, the Court order allowed the War Department to take possession of the acquired tracts upon deposit of designated funds with the Court.

The state leased its land to the War Department at no cost as provided in the 1939 contract. Additional land was leased for maneuver purposes making a total of 152,672 acres available for military training at Camp Blanding.

It was time to build the new camp.

Construction of the first building at Camp Blanding.

BUILDING THE CAMP

Planning the layout of the new camp began even before the first purchase of land was completed. The planning process began November 1, 1939, involving layout, utilities, streets and buildings. The plan included the following construction:

> 5 Caretaker houses
>
> 1 large galvanized iron and steel garage
>
> 2 galvanized iron and steel warehouses
>
> 2 Combination Administration Buildings, officers mess and officers latrine
>
> 4 Officers latrines
>
> 8 Battalion Enlisted Men's latrines
>
> 32 Mess halls
>
> 1 Officers Club

Progress was slow in the fall of 1939 because of a shortage of funds and a lack of expected and much-needed help. On October 3, 1939, Adjutant General Vivian Collins asked the State Road Department to prepare a topographical survey of seventy-five acres on the shores of Kingsley Lake with a contour interval of one foot. This survey was needed before construction of camp facilities. The Road Department replied by letter the next day that "The Road Board feels they should not be called upon to do this work." Despite another effort by Governor Fred P. Cone, the Road Board also declined to assist with preparation of twenty-five miles of clay road within the camp even though the roads were on state owned land and the work was a military necessity.

Governor Cone then suggested that an effort be made to secure a Civilian Conservation Corps camp in the area in order to utilize this kind of assistance in clearing land and preparing for construction. Senator Claude Pepper and Congressman Lex Green contacted the national Director of the C.C.C. program but Director Robert Fechner in a letter October 25, 1939, replied that "this organization does not undertake work on military reservations."

The first successful effort to get assistance with camp construction came from the Florida State Prison. Superintendent L. F. Chapman of the prison at Raiford agreed to furnish up to fifty inmates for this work provided the Armory Board paid the salaries of two guards for the period of the work. Each salary was seventy dollars per month.

The Adjutant General also was successful in getting significant help from the Works Projects Administration (WPA) in installing water and sewer lines; in construction of fences, roads and streets; in the construction of four mess halls, and in general beautification of the Camp site. After that initial work, the WPA worked on construction of the Rifle Range and an officer's recreation building. With assistance from these sources, work got underway to build the new camp.

The Adjutant General's Report for the years 1939 and 1940 provided detailed information that the $400,000 received by the Armory Board from the sale of Camp Foster was expended as follows at the new camp:

Purchase of 28,200 acres of land	$197,000.00
Water system	$ 13,327.00
Sewerage system	$ 25,129.97
Electric and telephone system	$ 8,051.04
Architects and Engineers	$ 9,796.65
Buildings	$126,879.14
Roads, streets and clearing	$ 16,620.48
Fence and miscellaneous	$ 3,195.70
	——————————
	$400,000.00

The contract between the state and the War Department provided that the new camp would provide "essential facilities adequate to accommodate one Regiment of Infantry (to) be completed by July 1, 1940." This was to provide training for National Guard units of Florida and other Southern states. However, it was clear to the Armory Board that the facility would be much more valuable if it were constructed to accommodate an infantry brigade. At that time the army tables of organization were based on the old "square division" consisting of two infantry brigades of two regiments each. Thus the layout called for two equal size regimental areas divided by a parade ground in the middle, accommodating twice the number of troops required by the contract with the War Department.

Behind each regimental headquarters building the plan called for a row of administrative buildings, mess halls and latrines. National Guard troops coming for summer training were to be housed in tents adjacent to these buildings.

A letter from Fourth Corps Area Headquarters in Atlanta November 7, 1939, suggested that the Adjutant General "consider where you would put the various elements of a division." This would again double the number of troops to be accommodated because a division consisted of two infantry brigades and two artillery brigades plus a large contingent of support elements. Before the end of the year 1940, news would be received that Camp Blanding would be required to house two army divisions for training. This would make the camp more than eight times the size contemplated in the September 1939 contract because of the need for a substantial station complement including a hospital.

When it was decided in 1940 that Camp Blanding would be the training site for National Guard troops called to active duty for a year, decision was made to house the troops in hutments. These were wooden frames and wooden floors covered by pyramidal tentage and heated with a stove in each hutment.

As this work got underway the Armory Board exercised its right to salvage materials from Camp Foster. The only building that was not salvaged was the Navy Exchange. In an article on "The Genesis of Camp Blanding," Brigadier General Ralph W. Cooper, Jr. (Ret.) wrote that "WPA labor and Military Department personnel were used for the salvage operation and prisoners from the state penitentiary at Raiford were used for the clearing operation. Salvaged materials were moved from Camp Foster to the new site using military trucks driven by National Guard personnel....A water system and sewage system, including a small disposal plant, came into being and electricity was furnished by the Florida Power & Light Company. A telephone line was installed from the camp to the Starke Telephone Company at Starke. Construction was by Military Department personnel and consisted of a pole line carrying two pairs phantomed to provide three trunk lines."

Before the end of 1939 the new camp got its name. Meeting in Orlando November 10, 1939, the Florida National Guard

Officers Association recommended the name Camp Albert H. Blanding. The Armory Board concurred, and Governor Cone approved the name in a letter to the Adjutant General December 14, 1939. Formal announcement was issued in General Orders No. 1, January 1, 1940, noting that "this designation is made as a mark of honor and in recognition of the distinguished military service rendered to the state and nation by Major General Albert H. Blanding, Florida National Guard." (See Appendix p. 203 for biography of General Blanding.)

As the New Year began, work was going forward with heightened enthusiasm and attracting increased public interest. Both the Florida National Guard and the Regular Army began a program to keep the public informed of the work at Camp Blanding and plans for the future as far as security considerations allowed.

Speaking to the Rotary Club of Starke at a cottage on Sand Hill Lake (now known as Lowry Lake) in December 1939, Brigadier General Sumter L. Lowry, commander of the 56th Field Artillery Brigade of the Florida National Guard, displayed maps and described the planned camp facilities. He commented that "I do not think the people of your community fully realize yet just what this development is going to mean to Starke."

That same week Col. Byron Bushnell, executive officer of the 116th Field Artillery, and Major Patrick Shea, Regular Army senior instructor for artillery in Florida, made a similar presentation to the Rotary Club of Jacksonville.

The *Bradford County Telegraph* diligently covered progress of construction and its impact on the county and the town of Starke. In its issue of March 15, 1940, the *Telegraph* reported "the sandhill and scrub oak area around the east side of Kingsley Lake is beginning to take on a vastly changed appearance...the air is now filled with the static of rapping hammers, steel riveting machines, and the hum of government trucks."

"What the gigantic new development will mean to Bradford County in dollars and cents is impossible to estimate, but it's fun to speculate just the same," said the article. But the *Telegraph's* speculation was far too low: "the possibility that 10,000 men might be encamped in the area."

The same article reported that Gallespi Construction Company of Jacksonville had a $60,000 contract to build three concrete and steel structures, a garage and shop building, a federal warehouse and a state warehouse. It also reported Robinson Construction Company of Haines City had a $20,000 contract for construction of ten mess halls and kitchens, and Gray Well & Pump Company of Jacksonville had a contract for a well and pump house.

While this work was going on, it was not contemplated that Florida National Guard troops would use Camp Blanding for their regular summer camps in 1940. The first use by a National Guard unit was on Monday, August 4, 1940, when the 116th Field Artillery Regiment fired its 75 mm artillery pieces on the range near Sand Hill Lake. The honor of firing the first round was accorded to Brigadier General Sumter L. Lowry, commander of the 56th Field Artillery Brigade of which the 116th regiment was a part. General Lowry was one of the early leaders in the development of Camp Blanding.

This artillery unit and other elements of the Florida National Guard participated that summer in maneuvers in Louisiana in lieu of summer training in Florida.

The *Bradford County Telegraph* issue of June 7, 1940, displayed on its front page photographs of work on the buildings referred to in the March 15 issue to "give a faint idea of the rapid progress that is being made at Camp Blanding."

But this progress was painfully slow compared to the tempo that would prevail soon when the entire post was leased to the War Department as contemplated in the September 1939 contract. The Armory Board formally turned the entire post over to the War Department December 1, 1940. The federal government then purchased an additional 40,000 acres for ranges and training areas and leased additional land for maneuver purposes bringing the total to more than 150,000 acres.

By mid-year 1940 the War Department announced that Camp Blanding would house the 31st Division of National Guard troops from Florida, Alabama, Louisiana and Mississippi when the division was called to active duty for one year of training. The division was ordered to active duty effective November 25, 1940. To get ready for these troops the Quartermaster Corps was assigned the mission of converting the partly sandy, partly swampy land into a usable campsite. Quartermaster construction men wrote extensively about the swamp conditions, but Lieutenant General S.D. Embick, commander of the United States Army Fourth Corps Area, kept the work going just as planned.

Even though the formal lease of state owned property to the federal government had not yet been signed, General Embick wrote the Adjutant General September 9, 1940, that "due to the recent developments in the mobilization plans this Headquarters finds it necessary to send an advance detachment of regular troops to Camp Blanding on September 15, 1940, to assume custody and begin preparations for the subsequent arrival of National Guard troops to be inducted into federal Service at an early date." General Embick noted that delay in signing the lease was "due to unavoidable legal difficulties" and expressed to Adjutant General Vivian Collins his "full appreciation for your excellent cooperation."

Pressure on construction work further increased when the War Department revealed plans for Camp Blanding to house the 43rd Infantry Division of National Guard troops from Maine, Vermont, Connecticut and Rhode Island when they were called to active duty for one year of training. This division was ordered to duty effective February 24, 1941.

This period experienced all the hectic ingredients of rapid wartime construction. The principal contractor was Starrett Brothers & Eken, a successful northern company that was on unfamiliar ground in Florida. Northern labor unions moved south and created tensions with independent southern labor. The pressure was on to build the facilities before the troops arrived.

The contractor needed 7,000 carpenters to begin the construction but nowhere near that number was available. He adopted the first of several innovative solutions: stationing experienced carpenters alongside the novices so that beginners could learn by doing. He then set up a system to pre-cut sections of mess halls at the sawmill and lumberyard. By this method a standard mess hall could be cut to size in the lumberyard in ten minutes and erected at the camp on its foundation in twenty-five minutes.

In his recollection fifty years later, Julian K. Wood of Bagdad, KY, who spent his entire thirty-nine months of army service at Camp Blanding, said "anybody who could use a hammer and drive a nail could get a job."

However, progress was too slow to meet War Department demands. Responsibility was shifted from the Quartermaster Corps to the Army Corps of Engineers Jacksonville District. This proved successful and enabled Secretary of War Henry L. Stimson to testify before the Truman Committee of the United States Senate that projects allocated to the Corps of Engineers "have been actively and efficiently prosecuted and are generally meeting the requirements of their scheduled completion dates."

The tempo of the work was well expressed before the Truman Committee by L. B. McLeod, owner of an Orlando construction company. He said: "I worked harder the first three months than I ever worked in my life, trying to find equipment somewhere in the country available. As a result, we rented equipment of every description that we could from sixteen other owners than ourselves....We went in there to do a job, to do it in a hurry, and put this defense program over with every ounce that we could put forth."

Writing for a publication of the 43rd Division before its mobilization, Colonel R. H. Kelley, commander of Camp Blanding in early 1941, assured the men of what they would find in Florida:

> Starting from scratch—a wilderness of scrub oak, palmetto, dense shrubbery and pine trees— Camp Blanding in less than six months time is a growing community with a population soon to rank fourth in the state of Florida. This miracle of accomplishment is evidence of high-pressure methods due to the great National Defense emergency. To make this evolution possible giant bulldozers have leveled broad expanses, forty-one miles of sewer pipes have been laid, five water tanks erected with a respective capacity of 1,000,000 gallons, 500,000 gallons and 100,000 gallons each, fifty-five miles of main roads and 350 to 500 miles of secondary roads and trails constructed, thirty-three miles of lead covered cables laid for telephone communication and over 1,150 structures built for various utilities and purposes. Camp

Blanding is termed in army vernacular a 'tent
camp' and as such approximately 11,000 tents
have been erected, all pyramidal, both for officers and enlisted men. These have the advantage over small wall tents of being heated by
Sibley stoves. Each houses one to three officers
or five to six enlisted men comfortably."

He also told the 43rd about the recreation and athletic
facilities available to them, the educational opportunities at
the University of Florida and the hospital to be staffed with
ninety-five doctors and 240 nurses. Actually the hospital staff
became much larger than that. Camp Blanding had to be
ready for arrival of the two National Guard divisions, and
it was.

Construction nearing completion of the first buildings at
Camp Blanding. The buildings still stand on both sides of
the parade ground.

BOOMTOWN U. S. A.

By the summer of 1940 citizens of Starke were beginning to realize that their little city was about to undergo major changes with the coming of a big military installation. The *Bradford County Telegraph* faithfully reported developments, alerted the community to what was coming and explained the economic impact. As part of the 50th anniversary commemoration of World War II, the newspaper published a series of historical articles in the paper in 1991 and 1992.

On August 8, 1940, the same week that General Lowry pulled the lanyard on the first artillery round ever fired at Camp Blanding, the *Telegraph* announced the first major business expansion in Starke. DeWitt C. Jones, former mayor of Starke and owner of the Starke Coca-Cola Bottling Company, announced expansion of his plant from a capacity of 24,000 bottles to 112,000 bottles per day. He leased the building next door to add 45,000 square feet to his plant, ordered 57,600 new bottles, 2,400 new delivery crates and four new trucks.

Jones said, "If the men and officers don't have access to our facilities in their recreation period, we will at the very start receive a black eye and they'll spend all their money and recreation time elsewhere."

The *Telegraph* commented: "A view of Starke's uptown street corners after nine o'clock the past few nights show dozens of men in uniform standing around idly for lack of anything to do. The young men can't even buy a picture post-card and a stamp to write to distant relatives and friends. And this with only 800 men now stationed at the camp." Adjutant General Vivian Collins warned the Starke Chamber of Commerce to anticipate a demand for 2,000 to 4,000 rooms for officers and senior non-commissioned officers (usually referred to as non-coms or NCOs) who would bring their families when the units came to Camp Blanding. The August 23, 1940 issue of the *Telegraph* reported the War Department had asked for $3,760,000 for new construction at Camp Blanding. This kind of news alerted the real estate business. Frank Hollingsworth, a local realtor, called the *Telegraph* office to order option contracts, a legal form not used in Starke since the near-forgotten boom days of 1925—26.

Developments came rapidly. The newly revived Chamber of Commerce was besieged with inquiries about potential locations for new businesses. Congressman Lex Green, who already owned Call Street property, planned another building there, Jim Forest bought a lot for $2,000 for a restaurant, Sistrunk's pool room and the A & P were enlarged, and Mina Manassa Grady planned to erect a 1,000 seat deluxe theater.

Even before arrival of the mobilized National Guard troops, the last three months of 1940 brought an enormous influx of construction workers with the mission to have the camp ready for occupancy by troops in ninety days. If accomplished, this would make Camp Blanding a true "ninety-day wonder." The federal government exerted maximum pressure on all concerned, and Starke was almost overwhelmed.

Real estate changed hands rapidly and more construction plans were announced. Freeman Register announced construction of an L-shaped building to be leased to a New York firm for a recreation center with six bowling alleys, pool tables, a restaurant and lounge for service members.

The city of Starke began a major clean-up effort to present the best possible appearance to newcomers. Newly elected Mayor N.D. (Noon) Wainwright, Jr., said the town had to be ready to provide food and shelter for 5,000 workers who would arrive in two weeks.

Soon Starke became known as "Boomtown U. S. A.," as it rapidly took on the trappings of a big city. R.G. Kidd and E.C. Long were granted a franchise to operate a taxicab service. The rates were fifteen cents anywhere in Starke and one dollar for a carful to Kingsley Lake.

The *Telegraph* issue of September 27, 1940 had this front-page headline:

STARKE IS JUMPING
OUT OF THE RUTS!
Citizens Rub Their Eyes At
Phenomenal Changes
Now Taking Place

Construction workers came in even greater numbers than the *Telegraph* anticipated, and the housing problems were acute. Some workers with families resorted to sleeping on the ground with leaves and feed sacks as cover. The newspaper reported one man found a hog pen, which he covered with sacks and made it his family's, home, sleeping, cooking and eating there.

Such overcrowding brought health problems. The State Health Department condemned the estimated 150 outdoor surface toilets in the city. They were to be replaced by cement and cypress wood units being constructed by the WPA.

The influx of families with construction workers brought problems to the school system. The Bradford County School Board adopted an emergency tuition fee of $5.00 per month for each child entering school from other states.

The *Telegraph* said the boom was like a gold rush without any gold but with plenty of $2.00 bills. These bills were used to pay off workers at the campsite. Because they were relatively rare, this was a way of demonstrating to local people the economic impact of a big operation, civilian or military. Substantially all the economic activity in Starke revolved around the Camp Blanding projects. While the Seaboard Air Line Railroad and the Southern Railway were constructing spur tracks to Camp Blanding, 150 carloads of building material lined up on sidings waiting to go to Camp Blanding.

Real estate transactions continued at a rapid pace. The *Telegraph* illustrated this hectic pace with the story of Kathleen Hall who was forced to move her Gem Lunch Room three times in three weeks. Her first move was to make way for the City Barber Shop, which was moving to make way for the expansion of Canova Pharmacy. She moved into a vacant store but received notice two days later that another concern had a previous lease on the building. She then moved into Congressman Green's building on the corner of Call and Court but soon got word that building was being torn down for construction of a new building. Her third move was into space formerly occupied by the Chamber of Commerce.

When the construction work force reached a peak of 21,000, more health problems were inevitable. Thousands of migrant families were homeless, and the problem became more severe when employment declined as the construction phase wound down. Health officials faced the impossible task of inoculating 21,000 workers against typhoid. All the local welfare agencies were striving earnestly to collect surplus food for the homeless.

Starke's own National Guard unit received its orders and was mobilized November 25, 1940, for one year of duty at Camp Blanding. First Lt. T.T. Long commanded the unit. The other officer was Second Lt. Richard Kidd. The Starke men who answered this call were Elmo Struth, James Dennis, Vincent (Sam) Alvarez, Al Kay Carlisle, Robert Dobbs, Robert Long, Morris Jackson, Walter Jackson, Walter Johnson, Owen Baker, John Crews, Theodore Goodge, L. H. Harper, Edwin Malone, Zach Myrick, Sam Simpson, George Silcox, L.O. Jones, A.W. Anderson Jr., Tracy Baker, Rudolph Andrews, William A. Edwards, Thomas (Cliff) Hazen and Demetrious Zacharias. Many of these men or their families are familiar names in Starke more than fifty years later.

Christmas 1940 was the biggest ever for merchants of Starke but the boom was marred on Christmas Eve by a sudden blackout. The *Telegraph* said the power outage was a signal that Starke's municipal power plant was cracking under the terrific overload to which it had been subjected since mid-October. Despite the power troubles, merchants were happy with their profits. Deposits in the Florida Bank at Starke for the three days after Christmas were up 100 percent over the previous year.

Starke postmaster Fred F. Stump told the *Telegraph* he had not completed calculation of postal receipts but December stamp sales were two or three hundred percent above last Christmas, and general delivery mail was up a thousand percent.

Boomtown U. S. A. received national media attention with articles in *Time, Saturday Evening Post, Colliers* and several metropolitan newspapers, especially in the areas from which the National Guard troops would come to Camp Blanding. These troops would begin arriving before the end of 1940, and

Starke would see a resurgence of its economic boom as the soldiers and their families spent their money in Starke.

A state census in 1945, the last year of the war, showed permanent effect on the population of Starke. From a population of 1,486 in 1940, the number of "permanent" residents increased by 43.5 percent to 2,131. In addition to these figures the census enumerator said there were 2,089 soldiers, their wives and children living in Starke, making the population 4,220.

Dignitaries frequently visited the high priority construction project at Camp Blanding in 1941. This photo was taken near the lumber mill.

ARRIVAL OF TROOPS

The 31st Division Comes First

The first major unit to arrive at Camp Blanding for its one year of training was the 31st Division, known as the "Dixie Division" because it was made up of National Guard units from Florida, Alabama, Mississippi and Louisiana. One of its regiments was the 124th Infantry of the Florida National Guard, which also furnished the 116th Field Artillery, and several companies of the 106th Engineers, the 106th Quartermaster Regiment and the 106th Medical Regiment. The division had what was then the standard organization of a "square division" with four infantry regiments and four artillery regiments.

The division was inducted into federal service at hometowns on November 25, 1940. The division was notified it would be stationed at Camp Blanding, sent advance detachments to the new camp and received word from the advance party that troop movements to Camp Blanding could begin in early December. A popular song among mobilized Guardsmen and draftees was "Goodbye, dear, I'll be back in a year, little darling," but later events would change the year to "the duration."

The 124th Infantry arrived on December 20, and the entire division was assembled at Camp Blanding by December 22. The troops were not happy with what they found in their areas. This is understandable as the most optimistic date for completion of such an enormous construction project to accommodate a division was January 1, 1941. Also, it made a dreary Christmas season.

In their unit history after the war ended, the division historian wrote that "Men unloaded from troop trains on barren sand, often in a steady rain, to find that their company areas consisted of a plot of acreage with only a few tent frames for housing facilities and a less than half complete mess hall. Few bathhouses or latrines were completed. Canvas tents and cots were scarce. In addition to these handicaps, Dixie Division soldiers found that contrary to what some had expected, the weather was cold and unpleasant. Rain fell almost incessantly."

Undoubtedly this account was a bit of an exaggeration, as was a statement that "parts of the camp had an elevation of 145 feet above sea level" while Kingsley Lake had an elevation of 175 feet, "resulting in complete inundation of part of the camp during heavy rains." There was not a thirty-foot difference in elevation anywhere in the cantonment area. Recollections later by the 1940 camp commander Col. R.H. Kelley explained that a dry, flat area had been prepared for the 31st but it had rained severely for days just before their train rolled in. The drainage ditches had not yet been dug, and that was why the men found their area covered with water.

Nevertheless, members of the 31st showed their adaptability and esprit de corps by pitching in to help construction workers finish the necessary tasks. Soldiers who had skills as carpenters, electricians or plumbers worked alongside the contractors' civilian employees. The historian recorded that "in a short time company streets appeared where only sand had been."

Before the year ended, the War Department had alerted Camp Blanding to expect the 43rd Division to occupy the other half of the two-division size camp nearing completion. The 43rd troops consisted of National Guard units of Maine, Vermont, Connecticut and Rhode Island. This meant Camp Blanding would have one division from New England and one from the Deep South. The two camp areas would be divided by the parade ground. Naturally, the space between the two became known as the Mason-Dixon Line. This gave rise to the street names on the post. The four main avenues parallel to Kingsley Lake were named Alabama, Connecticut, Florida and Maine. Cross streets in each area were given names from cities in their own areas.

The 43rd Division would not be ordered to active duty until February 24, 1941. The 31st division was ready for its training to begin on January 2, 1941. However, the soldiers had a few more tasks to make the Camp Blanding facilities ready for the intensive training the division needed. Roads to the ranges and training areas had to be made adequate to take convoys of trucks and marching columns of men. Some of the training facilities themselves needed more work, so 31st Division soldiers dug trenches for grenade courses, prepared moving target ranges for machine gun fire and generally brought the training facilities up to standard.

The division, far below its authorized strength at mobilization, received its first draftees in late February when 7,143 recruits from the division's four states arrived. These men had to start with basic training. Selected officers and non-coms first assigned them to replacement companies in each regiment for training. Before the end of March, division commander Major General John C. Persons ordered a thorough field inspection covering everything learned up to date. After eight weeks of their first military training, the new recruits were assigned to their units for advanced training.

With these new soldiers in their units alongside the veteran National Guard men, all units began an intensive three-month training period in April to exercise all echelons in their combat operations up to division level. During this training period General Persons issued a practice alert on the night of May 15, 1941. Five hours after the orders were issued, all units of the division had cleared the gates with foot soldiers marching and motorized columns following. In accord with the division's pre-arranged plans, all units set up completely for field operations. They were inspected and returned to camp. It was a successful exercise. Key non-commissioned officers of units throughout the division were given specialized advanced training in map reading, night observation, night patrolling, motorized patrolling and intelligence work of all kinds.

In a preview of what would come to Camp Blanding fifty years later, the 31st Division conducted an urban warfare exercise in May. They assaulted the false-front town of "Thompsonville" in the face of simulated machine gun and sniper fire, air attacks and other tricks of this kind of fighting, then engaged in hand-to-hand street fighting to take and hold the village. (Similar exercises are held at Camp Blanding today with new and better weapons at a recently constructed city of "Smithville.")

Still another training exercise for the men of the 31st was a sixty-mile march to set up and operate the division completely without immediate access to the post. This took place in July 1941 when General Persons ordered the division to march sixty-miles to Ocala National Forest. This was accomplished well within the time allotted after which the division engaged in three days of maneuvers in the dense forest. After a short rest, the men were paid and they marched back to Camp Blanding in three days. After this exercise the merchants of "Boomtown U. S. A." in Starke did a flourishing business with the relaxing soldiers.

The 31st Division was then ready for the big army maneuvers in Louisiana in August. Their historian writes that for these maneuvers "morale was excellent and physical condition of the men was at an all time peak."

The 43rd Division Arrives

President Franklin Roosevelt signed the formal order mobilizing the 43rd Division January 14, 1941, although members had been alerted earlier. Their mobilization was effective February 24, 1941. Like the 31st Division, the 43rd was organized as a "square division" with four infantry regiments.

The division was commanded by Major General Morris B. Payne, of New London, Conn. Its units proceeded from their home armories to Camp Blanding, and the division was in its area by March 19, 1941. Since the Corps of Engineers had three more months to prepare for the arrival of this division than for the 31st, the complaints were fewer. The men of the 43rd found the life style of North Florida different from New England. Many found this to be favorable and later moved to Florida.

Upon arrival at Camp Blanding in March 1941, the 43rd Division began a thirteen-week training program much like that of the 31st Division with tactical problems and exercises ranging from small units to brigade versus brigade. Naturally an element of competition between the two divisions added zest to the training, and an element of good-natured bantering. The story goes that some troops from Louisiana were railing at the Yankees across the "Mason Dixon Line" in Cajun French. The men of the 43rd then rounded up some 103rd Infantrymen who replied in the French dialect of northern Maine. It is uncertain whether either group understood the other, but it was all in good fun. Not all encounters were in good fun, however. Although few and isolated, there were incidents of "re-fighting the Civil War," including a legendary clash between a Texan and a Brooklynite with reported loss of an ear by one of the combatants.

During this training period both officers and enlisted men were permitted to spend week-ends with their families in Starke, Gainesville, Green Cove Springs, Jacksonville, St. Augustine, Palatka and Keystone Heights. The unmarried men and those whose families remained at home found Starke, the nearest town, a hospitable center for civilian food, movies and other entertainment. The explosive growth, bringing in thousands of unattached young men—construction workers and soldiers—fueled some less desirable development. A honky-tonk community sprung up outside the gates on the road to Starke. It aroused vigorous action by the camp command with bulldozers playing a role when "off limits" didn't accomplish the desired result.

In another similarity to the 31st Division, the 43rd was below authorized strength. By this time Camp Wheeler, near Macon, Georgia, was in operation as an Infantry Replacement Training Center. Draftees who had received thirteen weeks of basic training at Camp Wheeler were sent to Camp Blanding to join the 43rd Division. By arrangement between General Persons and Brigadier General John H. Hester, commander of Camp Wheeler, the draftees were assigned to organizations originating in or near the cities from which the new men came into service wherever this was possible. Older members agreed this had helped in assimilation of the new men just as had been the case in the 31st. Nevertheless, many came from other parts of the country, and soon the 43rd Division was composed of men from virtually every state in the union.

The division's intensive training program ended in early July, and a liberal leave and furlough policy allowed many officers and enlisted men to return to New England to visit their families. They had to return for the division to prepare for participation in the big army maneuvers in Louisiana in August and September.

Off to Maneuvers, Then Back to Blanding

Both divisions departed in early August for maneuvers in Louisiana. The men of the 31st were passing through and training in their home areas. Wherever possible their itineraries were planned to go through hometowns where civic organizations and other groups of well wishers greeted the troops and offered entertainment and other courtesies. Many men had brief visits with relatives.

For the men of the 43rd it was a new experience. It was the most rugged training under simulated combat conditions that these troops had seen. They learned lessons here that would turn out to be valuable in their future campaigns in jungles of the South Pacific. The Louisiana environment was similar to what they would face. They encountered chiggers, redbugs and ticks along with dust or mud in the Louisiana lowlands.

Joseph E. Zimmer, who later wrote a history of the 43rd Division, noted that the Louisiana experience made the men appreciate Camp Blanding. He wrote, "Up until time for departure for Louisiana, Camp Blanding had not been accepted too enthusiastically by the New Englanders as a foster home. However, it may be recorded without contradiction that the prospect of returning there to its semi-permanent

quarters and mess halls, not to mention steaming hot showers, was welcomed with a great deal of enthusiasm." Both divisions recorded their experience in the maneuvers as
demonstrations of their prowess and indicators of their future success in combat.

For the men of the 31st Division, their commander General Persons seized the opportunity to grant seven-day leaves
and furloughs to members of the Louisiana and Mississippi
units before they left the maneuver area. Thus they were able
to visit their families at minimum expense. Alabama and
Florida unit members were granted furloughs upon their
return to Camp Blanding, one-third at a time until all had
been given the privilege.

General Persons insisted that each man must pass a rigid
personal inspection before departure and must show evidence
that he had the necessary transportation. Hitchhiking was
expressly prohibited.

Back at Camp Blanding the army began issuing complete
wool uniforms to all enlisted men. This was in anticipation of
the next maneuvers to be held in North Carolina and South
Carolina in October. Each man received a new field jacket
(valued then at seven dollars), a wool coat, shirt and trousers.

Dances and open house social functions were offered to
the men at the hostess house, as the service clubs had not yet
been completed. Starke and Green Cove Springs always offered the attractions of movies and restaurants with food
served civilian style.

Both divisions went through inspections and replenishment
of supplies and equipment before the October maneuvers.
The 43rd Division gained a new commander on October 8,
1941, when Major General John H. Hester succeeded Major
General Payne. General Hester was already known to many
in the division because he had commanded the Infantry Re-

placement Training Center at Camp Wheeler from which a large number of replacements had come to the 43rd.

Both divisions moved out in late October for the second major army maneuvers of the year, this time in South Carolina and North Carolina with much colder weather than they had experienced in Louisiana. They returned to Camp Blanding in late November, and the commanders of both divisions told their troops they had performed well and brought credit to their divisions.

Then came December 7, 1941, and the Japanese attack on Pearl Harbor. The United States declared war on Japan the next day and on Germany and Italy two days later.

Construction leaders walked a section of the railroad at a twenty-six-foot fill on Camp Blanding while construction was underway in 1940.

Typical pose of three soldiers outside their mess hass. probably on a Sunday in August 1944. Left to right—Owen Elliott, Robert Engle and Robert Hass.

WORLD WAR II BEGINS

The Japanese attack on Pearl Harbor December 7, 1941 brought many changes to life at Camp Blanding and the neighboring communities. The United States faced formidable enemies in Europe and the Pacific. Military training at Camp Blanding, already intensive in nature, had to be pressed even more vigorously to get the two National Guard divisions ready for combat as soon as possible.

The 31st Division canceled all leaves and furloughs, but upon further consideration the Army's Fourth Corps Area authorized furloughs for up to twenty-five percent of the men of the 31st Division. The rest of the division continued to prepare for whatever orders might be received. New orders came soon. The division was ordered to send units to defend the Atlantic Seaboard. Dixie Division troops took positions at strategic points from Wilmington, N.C., to Key West, FL. This was a brief assignment, and the division was re-assembled at Camp Blanding in January 1942 with orders to proceed by truck cross-country to Camp Bowie, Texas. The 31st would exchange places with the 36th Division, a Texas National Guard unit. The 31st left Blanding on February 23, 1942.

The 43rd Division had similar experiences in December 1941. Furloughs for Christmas were allowed, and special trains were arranged to take these men to their home cities in New England. Everyone knew it was no longer one-year of federal service but they were in "for the duration." The army was creating new divisions, and the 43rd was called on to supply officer and NCO cadres on several occasions. This necessitated specialized training for personnel replacing those who had gone as cadres.

The first unit of the 43rd to be deployed was the 102nd Infantry, which left Camp Blanding in January 1942 for extended service in the Pacific. This regiment would never rejoin the division because the standard division organization was changed from the "square" division to a triangular configuration with three infantry regiments. This left the 43rd Division with its three regiments being the 103rd, the 169th and the 172nd.

On February 8, 1942, the 43rd received orders for a permanent change of station to Camp Shelby, Mississippi, where the triangularization reorganization was completed. The division left Camp Blanding February 14, 1942.

The nearby town of Starke reacted on December 7, 1941, with all-out patriotic support for the war effort and for the troops at Camp Blanding. The next issue of the *Bradford County Telegraph* reported the news this way: "Packed with soldiers and six miles from the second largest training camp in the United States, Starke nevertheless accepted calmly the resolution passed by Congress" declaring war on Japan. Guards were posted twenty-four hours a day at the local water and power plants, and Florida Power and Light Company was reported "closely guarding its main power lines, especially in the vicinity of Camp Blanding." Page one of the newspaper reported the national Red Cross campaign to raise $50 million. The local chapter's quota was $1,250. The Red Cross said chapters could retain fifteen percent of the funds raised to support local efforts.

Operations at Camp Blanding went on a twenty-four-hour basis with anti-aircraft protection (as well as the units could provide), vehicle dispersion and accelerated training tempo. The *Telegraph* reported that Camp Blanding was blacked out at night, so "cooks waited till dawn before being able to start breakfast for 40,000 soldiers," but also noted that "declaration of war apparently does little to dampen the spirits of Blanding's soldier population. Starke's movie houses and beer parlors are crowded with khaki-lads, apparently just as carefree as they were a week ago."

Russell Kay, a prominent Florida newspaperman, wrote in the same issue that "America today is aroused as never before in her history, her wrath is righteous and her cause just. Now she understands, realizes she has a job to do and she will grimly and determinedly set about doing it."

The editor of the *Telegraph* commented in an editorial "Now that the crisis is here, citizens of Bradford and every other county in the state and nation will rise to the task and each will do his part. The local Defense Council has already snapped into action with an important meeting called for this week."

This unified spirit of support for the war effort continued throughout the conflict in Starke as in the rest of the country.

This photo shows sixty-one people at work on a cold storage unit roof slab at CampBlanding in January 1941.

NEW DIVISIONS ARRIVE FOR TRAINING

The 36th Division

With departure of the 31st and 43rd divisions, Camp Blanding was ready to receive two more divisions for training before deployment to the war zones. The 36th Division of Texas National Guard troops arrived February 19, 1942. Like its two predecessors at Camp Blanding, the 36th Division had received a large number of men from the Selective Service System to fill its ranks. They came from all over the country, but the people of Texas always regarded the 36th as their own.

Like the other divisions the 36th also had participated in the Louisiana maneuvers in 1941 and was converted to a triangular division before the end of 1941. The division began its move by truck from Camp Bowie to Camp Blanding on Valentine's Day, February 14, 1942. This motor march was unpleasant to say the least. Heavy rains fell frequently. Many trucks were stuck in the mud of east Texas, and manpower was used to get them rolling when the trucks' winches couldn't do the job. With this kind of determination the 36th Division reached Camp Blanding on February 19, 1942.

Like all other old divisions of the active army and the National Guard, the 36th was called on to supply cadres for the formation of new divisions. At Camp Blanding the division received Selective Service replacements from Ohio, Kentucky, Tennessee and West Virginia. This process continued and eventually the 36th included men from every state in the union.

Taking advantage of Kingsley Lake, the men of the 36th had their first amphibious training. They also practiced new expedients for stream crossings and swimming with and without equipment. Camp Blanding also afforded the opportunity for live fire exercises. One of the unit historians described their experience this way: "We trained always; more marches...more heat...more sweat...twenty-five miles per day with equipment...rain...mud...wind...sun. We were ready to take to the field again." He also wrote, "On weekends we visited Jacksonville, St. Augustine, Daytona Beach, Jacksonville Beach and Silver Springs." Starke and Green Cove Springs were always nearby with their hospitality and entertainment.

This intensive training at Camp Blanding lasted five months for men of the 36th Division. In early July the division left for the 1942 maneuvers in North Carolina. While on these maneuvers, the 36th Division received word that it would not return to Camp Blanding. It would instead make a permanent change of station to Camp Edwards, Mass., arriving there in August 1942.

THE 1ST DIVISION

The regular Army 1st Infantry Division arrived at Camp Blanding almost simultaneous with the 36th Division. Called in army circles the "Big Red One" because of the red number one on its shoulder patch, the 1st Division was the oldest division in the army. It had a long and distinguished combat history and established another such record in World War II.

In 1942 most of the officers and the enlisted men of the 1st Division were Regular Army. All were conscious of that distinction and proud of the traditions of their division. Many of the senior officers were West Pointers and many of the other officers and enlisted men were career soldiers. These regulars saw themselves as superior to draftees and made this distinction clear to all. The division arrived at Camp Blanding February 21, 1942, for inspections, verifications of equipment status and other preparation for overseas movement along with some final training before deployment.

Before the month was out, a troop train brought the division several hundred soldiers who had just completed basic training at Fort Bragg, NC. Most of them, but not all, were draftees. The regulars immediately established their position by assigning the new men to separate tables in the mess hall. One of the new men was William E. Faust who now lives in St. Augustine, FL. He was Regular Army but the Regulars did not know this until payday. The serial number of Regular Army members began with the digit one, and at pay-call Regular Army men were paid first. On his first payday at Camp Blanding, Faust's status became known. Thereafter, he was permitted to eat with the Regulars. Later he even got invited to have a few beers with some of the old soldiers.

At Camp Blanding Faust described the routine as "all business: drilling, overnight problems, rifle practice on the firing range, hikes, field stripping rifles, guard duty and more drilling." When the troops had free time on weekends, they usually headed for Starke. Members of the 36th Division, the Texas National Guard division, did likewise, leading to some off-post conflicts. The Texans tried to demand that everybody, including 1st Division men, stand at attention when the juke box played "Deep in the Heart of Texas." Hand-to-hand combat often resulted with the Texans on one side and the Big Red One ones on the other.

While at Blanding the 1st Division was inspected on May 1, 1942, by General George C. Marshall, United States Army Chief of Staff, and Field Marshal Sir John Dill of the British Army, a member of the Joint Chiefs of Staff of the Allies. When the division assembled on the parade ground, Faust remembers "we were shined and polished from top to bottom, head to toe, general to private." About this time some of the men, including Faust, were told they were eligible for ten-day furloughs, but the furloughs were canceled and the troops started packing, painting code numbers on equipment and getting ready for departure.

Three weeks after General Marshall's visit, the division departed May 22, 1942, for Fort Benning, GA, and soon thereafter to its combat role in North Africa and its long and distinguished combat service in Europe.

THE 29TH DIVISION

The next division to arrive at Camp Blanding was the 29th. This was another National Guard division with troops from Maryland, Virginia, Pennsylvania and the District of Columbia. The division had been mobilized February 3, 1941 at its hometown armories, then assembled February 13 at Fort Meade, Maryland. In sequence the division then trained at Fort Meade, participated in the Carolina maneuvers, then was converted to the triangular division configuration, just as the other divisions had experienced. Thereafter, the division moved to Camp A.P. Hill, then participated in more maneuvers in North Carolina.

After all these moves, men of the 29th welcomed a move in August to Camp Blanding where they enjoyed the comfort of the cantonment area, the warm weather, the opportunities to swim in Kingsley Lake and the hospitality of the nearby cities and towns.

The first disruption of this comfortable life came soon when the division was ordered to send its artillery battalions to Fort Sill, Oklahoma, for service with the Artillery School and also to send an infantry regiment to Fort Benning for the same type of duty at the Infantry School. Before either of these troops reached their destination, however, the 29th received orders to prepare immediately for overseas movement. Hectic days ensued with staff officers spending three days on the telephones recalling personnel who were on furlough as well as getting the advance party of artillerymen back from Fort Sill.

The division then conducted showdown inspections of every item of equipment, crated and packed organizational equipment and gave required inoculation shots to all personnel. All these tasks were completed expeditiously, and the 29th Division left Camp Blanding September 20 for its next station at Camp Kilmer, New Jersey, and departure overseas immediately thereafter.

THE 79TH DIVISION

The 79th Division was activated at Camp Pickett, VA, June 15, 1942, in ceremonies which stressed the division's distinguished record of gallantry in four major engagements of World War I. The division arrived at Camp Blanding September 1, 1942, for six months of intensive training. This was the beginning of the autumn months. Eugene Maurey, then Motor Officer of the 904th Field Artillery Battalion, recalls that the weather was hot in the day and cold at night with high humidity causing rust problems, especially for his motor maintenance tools.

Maurey, now a resident of Chicago, took every opportunity to teach his men to drive under adverse circumstances. He says "They were delighted. Not only the designated drivers were my target of instruction but all the young teenagers who had not yet learned to drive. At that time, a few years after the Great Depression when few had automobiles, about eighty percent of draftees could not drive an automobile."

Early in its stay at Camp Blanding, the 79th Division—like so many others—was called on to furnish a cadre for a new division. This left openings for promotions but also brought many new recruits and led to a third cycle of basic training for the 79th. It was boring for many, but Maurey thinks it contributed to the division's splendid combat record.

The division commander Major General I.T. Wyche stressed barge landing exercises on Kingsley Lake with explosions provided by the 304th Engineers. The division left Camp Blanding March 3, 1943 for the Tennessee maneuver area and then to the desert training center in California for further training before deployment to Europe.

THE 30TH DIVISION

The 30th Infantry Division traveled a rocky road for two years before it reached Camp Blanding. This National Guard division consisted of troops of Tennessee, North Carolina, South Carolina and Georgia. It was called to federal service for one year of training effective September 16, 1940. It spent two years training at Fort Jackson, S.C. and participated in Second Army maneuvers in 1941 in Tennessee and later the same year in maneuvers in North Carolina and South Carolina.

In 1942 the 30th Division went through the same reorganization as the other old divisions from the "square" division to the triangular division with three infantry regiments. Also in that year the 30th lost large numbers of men to cadres of new divisions, officer candidate schools and Army Air Forces training. During that summer also, the division's 118th Infantry Regiment and 115th Field Artillery Battalion had been pulled out and sent overseas as a combat team.

On September 12, 1942, Major General Leland S. Hobbs became the division commander. By that time the division had suffered a manpower loss of the equivalent of a full division of officers and men. Fillers began to arrive and the 119th Infantry and 197th Field Artillery Battalion were constituted to replace the departed 118th Infantry and 115th Field Artillery Battalion. But the division's manpower problems—not of their own making—continued when the 117th Infantry Regiment was sent to Fort Benning, GA., on September 13 for duty at the Infantry School and remained there until February 28, 1943.

The division was transferred to Camp Blanding for further unit training and arrived October 6, 1942. By this time fully two-thirds of the privates in the division had come directly from reception centers. Then the division had to initiate a new complete training program beginning with the usual thirteen weeks of basic individual training followed by another thirteen weeks of small unit training. Camp Blanding was the ideal spot for this training with all the facilities available, which had been successfully used in the same manner nearly two years earlier by the 31st and 43rd divisions.

In May 1943 the division artillery performed in outstanding fashion in firing tests at Camp Gordon, GA, while the rest of the division conducted intra-division field maneuvers near Lynchburg, Tenn. From this exercise the division moved on to two months of large-scale maneuvers with several other divisions.

It is to the credit of the 30th that, after so many reorganizations, it could perform so well in major army maneuvers and ultimately establish a distinguished combat record in Europe. The 30th Division did not return to Camp Blanding after the 1943 maneuvers but went on for further firing tests at Camp Atterbury, Indiana, and then to Boston for departure to Europe. The Division's last day of duty at Camp Blanding was May 30, 1943.

THE 66TH DIVISION

Departure of the 79th Division in March 1943 left space for another division at Camp Blanding. This time, rather than providing training facilities for an old division, Camp Blanding provided its facilities for the activation of an entirely new infantry division.

On April 15, 1943, the 66th Infantry Division was activated in a ceremony on the parade ground with the entire division present. Most of the men had received little, if any, initial training. At the activation ceremony, Major General H. F. Kramer, the new division's commander, promised the men a "stiff training program," and that's exactly what they got at Camp Blanding. He described it well when he told them the program's purpose was "to teach our troops how to kill and not be killed; to develop leadership and teamwork; to harden the officers and men mentally and physically, and to forge each link in the chain of command."

The division's cadre came from the 89th Division at Camp Carson, Colorado. As with other new divisions being activated, these cadre officers and NCOs attended specialist training to prepare them for responsibilities they had not experienced before.

Their experience at Camp Blanding was something new for these men who had never served before. For them it was tougher than for the National Guard men who had received training regularly on a part-time basis back in their home towns and knew what to expect at Camp Blanding. The men of the 66th made long marches in the Florida heat, spent long days on the firing ranges, ran obstacle courses and had some breaks for lectures on all the basic military subjects.

Writing the division's history after war's end, Siinto S. Wessman described their Camp Blanding experience this way: "They threw it at us hot and heavy and, although it was pretty tough at first, we soon got that feeling of well-trained men and took all the training in stride."

Jacksonville had a special attraction for the men of the 66th, and the 66th won the hearts of that city where it was called "Jacksonville's division." Their historian also records that other Florida cities and towns now hold fond memories for the men of the 66th.

All in all, the division's experience at Camp Blanding was militarily successful and pleasant during their off-duty time. But it came to an end in August when the division received orders to move to Camp Robinson in Little Rock, Arkansas. So the 66th Division departed Camp Blanding August 17, 1943, for more training, field maneuvers and eventual service in the European theater.

THE 63RD DIVISION

The 63rd Infantry Division became the second new division to be activated at Camp Blanding, just two months after activation of the 66th Division. The 63rd Division was formally activated on June 15, 1943. It was a textbook case in the selection and preparation of the cadre, activation, training and deployment of a new division, which established a long and distinguished record in combat.

At the activation ceremony Brig Gen. Louis E. Hibbs, the division commander, told members of the 63rd Division that "never before has there been an American unit of that name. This division starts, therefore, with no history....Your history lies before you."

The 63rd identified itself as the "Blood and Fire" division. In his activation remarks General Hibbs told his men "Your role is combat, nothing else." Referring to their shoulder patch, he said "Let the blood and fire you wear on your shoulder keep you reminded always that war is a bloody and vicious game....This emblem was designed to keep you reminded that you either kill your enemy or he kills you."

Copies of the division newspaper *Blood and Fire* were distributed to all personnel at the ceremony. The newspaper provided information about all commanders and other senior leaders of the division.

Following the ceremony General Hibbs declared a holiday so division members could enjoy all the recreation facilities of Camp Blanding. Transportation was provided to and from the beaches. Theaters were opened for matinees, softball and volleyball games were arranged and dances were held in the evening at Service Club No. 1 for enlisted men and at Building No. 2817 for the officers.

The thorough preparation for activation began in February with selection by the War Department of the senior commanders and the Chief of Staff, all of whom assembled in Washington for conferences in March. Nothing was left to chance in the process. The division commander and his senior staff went through a training program at the Command and General Staff College, Fort Leavenworth, KS in March and April. Commanders of subordinate units of the division went for similar training at the Infantry School, Field Artillery School and other schools of other branches of the service.

The 98th Infantry Division was the "parent division" for the 63rd although cadre officers and NCOs came from several other divisions and from Replacement Training Centers. The 98th Division supplied most of the cadre officers who became small unit commanders or staff officers at regiment and battalion level. The 98th also provided most of the non-commissioned officers around whom the division was to be built.

The first contingent to arrive at Camp Blanding was the division commander and his staff. They came on May 3 and were followed immediately by other officers for the subordinate units of the division. The first large group of enlisted cadre arrived May 8, including mess sergeants and cooks, military police and postal workers followed by drivers, maintenance personnel and the rest of the enlisted cadre. They were ready for the activation on June 15 and for the arrival of their troops for training.

Today members of the 63rd Division have mixed memories of their time at Camp Blanding. In one sense, it was frustrating because they never received the bulk of their personnel while at Camp Blanding. In another sense, it had positive overtones because it gave the cadre time for what one 63rd veteran called "more training than any other comparable group." It also provided more time for recreation. The cadre took full advantage of Kingsley Lake with swimming session two or three times a week. This entailed the "buddy" system; when the whistle blew, all "buddies" had to raise their hands. After swimming came the inevitable policing the shore of the lake.

The cadre had plenty to do getting ready for the expected filler troops. Officers and NCOs worked on tasks they would not normally perform. They repaired hutments and walks while doing all the normal chores of an army unit. Items of individual equipment flowed in to supply sergeants in mass. All had to be counted, sorted and stored away. Motor maintenance NCOs had to do the same with scores of items of maintenance as new two and one-half ton trucks arrived to replace old one and one-half ton trucks.

Meanwhile, specialized advanced training was in high gear for all cadre members, everything pointed toward readiness to receive several thousand personnel who never arrived at Camp Blanding. Regardless of their specialties, cadre members made twenty-five-mile hikes with full field equipment, endlessly practiced rifle marksmanship with dummy ammunition in the areas near their hutments and fired on the rifle ranges in an effort to qualify everybody in rifle marksmanship.

In addition to swimming in Kingsley Lake, cadre members converted an old barracks into an NCO Club, took advantage of the service clubs, movie theaters and other on-post entertainment as well as frequent trips to the city of Jacksonville. Several63rd Division veterans recalled "fond memories" of Camp Blanding. One said it was the "best army camp of my three year career." One veteran added ,"It made such an impression on me that I resolved to some day live in Florida." It took him twenty-three years to achieve that goal, but he lives in Florida today. Another Blanding "alumnus," now living in Florida year-round in retirement, put it this way in a round-robin letter to friends: "It took Odysseus ten years to return home from his war. It took me fifty years to return from mine."

The 63rd Division ended its short tour of duty at Camp Blanding August 22, 1943 when it departed by motor convoy to Camp Van Dorn, Mississippi, where it received its filler personnel, conducted its training and subsequently established its outstanding combat record in Europe.

NON-DIVISIONAL UNITS

Camp Blanding was home for many other units smaller than divisions during World War II. Its massive size and superior training facilities, particularly firing ranges, made it ideal for these units. These were commonly referred to as (Separate) or (Non-Divisional) units.

Some units were converted to (Separate) status when the old divisions were reorganized from the square format with four infantry regiments to the triangular format with three regiments. The artillery of these divisions was similarly reorganized, making some artillery regiments and battalions into separate units. In addition to these spin-offs from divisions, other non-divisional units of infantry, cavalry, field artillery, tank destroyers and engineers came to Camp Blanding.

508TH PARACHUTE INFANTRY

While the 79th and 30th Divisions were training at Camp Blanding, another unit was organized that would become a source of great pride to organizers of the Camp Blanding Museum and Memorial Park fifty years later.

The 508th Parachute Infantry was formally established at Camp Blanding on October 20, 1942. It had been in the planning stage for more than a month under Major Roy E. Lindquist who would be its commander. His task was to select the cadre, and he personally interviewed and selected each officer and enlisted member of the cadre from three sources: the 502nd Parachute Infantry, the Parachute School at Fort Benning and the 26th Infantry Division. From the beginning Major Lindquist was determined to build an elite unit. He wanted only men who believed the United States Army Parachutists were the best soldiers in the world. He selected the cadre on this basis plus, of course, the military qualifications.

Troop trains began delivering recruits to the 508th immediately after unit activation. Major Lindquist was promoted to lieutenant colonel, and he set high standards for the processing and screening of these recruits. Most were in good physical condition, and all were volunteers for parachute duty but only half could meet the strict qualifications the commander required for the 508th. The mental testing was particularly grueling for the new men. A board of officers conducted screening interviews in each battalion.

The regiment's strength of 2,300 officers and men was selected from 4,500 processed at Camp Blanding. Training began immediately with twelve-hour work days with an emphasis on physical conditioning. Mornings always began with a half-hour run followed by heavy calisthenics. Close order drill interspersed with military lectures completed the usual morning program. The afternoon always included another hour of physical hardening along with weapons drills and other elements of basic training. Just as they would do later at Jump School, men ran from one assignment to the next including trips to the mess hall. Even punishments for minor infractions were used to increase stamina, the device being an order to perform a set number of push-ups.

While they built their physical stamina and their *esprit de corps*, men of the 508th were qualifying on the ranges with weapons they had first seen at Camp Blanding. For Christmas 1942 the men were given enough time off to buy gifts in Jacksonville, then back to their training. Regimental parades were held about once a week. The commander wanted a smart-looking as well as highly trained unit. In this Colonel Lindquist achieved his goal of a unit of men who considered the 508th an elite organization. As proficiency increased the commander instituted company competition and offered streamers for the guidons of the company chosen best in weapons firing, close order drill and physical prowess. Another regimental contest was held for the best idea of a shoulder patch and a war cry. Sergeant Andrew J. Sklivis submitted the winning shoulder patch drawing of a parachuting red devil carrying a grenade and a Tommy Gun. The battle cry selected was "Diablo!"

By now the men were so eager to get to jump school at Fort Benning they began counting down the number of days before they would depart. February 3, 1943 became the magic date when the 1st Battalion of the 508th began its move to Fort Benning. The rest of the regiment followed in the next two days. Substantiating the quality of their physical training at Camp Blanding, the 508th was excused from the parachute school's first week, called the "A" Stage, devoted only to physical conditioning.

At Fort Benning, at its subsequent training and ultimately in its outstanding combat performance, the 508th proved itself worthy of all the hard work they endured at Camp Blanding.

102ND INFANTRY REGIMENT (SEPARATE)

This Connecticut National Guard regiment was part of the 43rd Infantry Division when it was mobilized and came to Camp Blanding in March 1941. For nearly a year it was part of the 43rd Division which participated in maneuvers as a "square" division. The 102nd, less most of its Third Battalion, was detached from the 43rd Division and moved to the Charleston Port of Embarkation January 15, 1942. It then deployed to Bora Bora Society Islands and subsequent assignments in the South Pacific. Its Companies K and M remained at Camp Blanding and were assigned to the 91st Infantry Regiment (Separate). Interestingly, the 102nd Infantry Regiment became a part of the 43rd Division again when the division was recalled for the Korean War.

91ST INFANTRY REGIMENT (SEPARATE)

The Third Battalion of this regiment was activated at Camp Blanding March 10, 1942 with troops of Companies K and M of the departed 102nd Infantry. The 91st Infantry departed Camp Blanding April 19, 1942 and was deployed in July to Ascension Island, a strategic base in the south Atlantic for movements to Africa. It remained there until the war ended, then moved to the Philippines.

124TH INFANTRY REGIMENT

The 124th Infantry was a Florida National Guard unit, the first element of the 31st Division to arrive at Camp Blanding in December 1940. It was part of the division until December 1941 when it was transferred to Fort Benning, GA, to serve as school demonstration troops for the Infantry School. It thus became the 124th Infantry Regiment (Separate) and remained so until it was inactivated in March 1944.

This inactivation was regarded in Florida as a tragic injustice. Governor Spessard L. Holland immediately appealed to the Secretary of War, writing that "its inactivation would be a severe blow to morale both in and outside of the service and arouse bitterness in the hearts of many of our citizens." He asked that corrective action be taken.

The governor's intercession was successful. The 124th Infantry was activated again April 5, 1944. This time the activation was in Australia using troops of the 154th Infantry Regiment, which was inactivated on the same day. Thus the 124th Infantry again became a part of the 31st Division.

Members of the Florida National Guard in the original 124th Infantry served throughout the world after their unit was inactivated.

156TH INFANTRY REGIMENT (SEPARATE)

Although United States Army records identify this unit as 156th Infantry Regiment (Separate), this Louisiana National Guard regiment came to Camp Blanding in December 1940 as part of the 31st Division. It was detached from the 31st Division in July 1944, after the move to Camp Bowie, Texas. It continued as a separate unit for the rest of the war, serving with various missions in Africa and Europe.

6TH CAVALRY REGIMENT (MECHANIZED)

Originally a part of the 3rd Cavalry Division, the 6th Cavalry Regiment (Horse/Mechanized) became a separate unit in 1939. It came to Camp Blanding from Fort Oglethorpe, GA, Feb. 18, 1942. It was redesignated 6th Cavalry Regiment (Mechanized) July 21, 1942. It left Camp Blanding Nov. 2, 1942, and deployed to Europe in late 1943.

631ST TANK DESTROYER BATTALION (S-P)

643RD TANK DESTROYER BATTALION (S-P)

774TH TANK DESTROYER BATTALION (S-P)

These three tank destroyer battalions were all activated at Camp Blanding December 15, 1941, just a week after the United States entered World War II. Many other tank destroyer units were activated at the same time at other posts throughout the country as the army was rapidly expanding.

The 631st and 643rd were organized with towed anti-tank guns, and both were converted to self-propelled in 1942. The 631st deployed to England in August 1944, and the 643rd deployed to France in September 1944. The 774th was organized as a heavy self-propelled battalion. In late 1943 it was converted to towed three-inch guns and deployed to Europe in June 1944.

74TH FIELD ARTILLERY BRIGADE

This Georgia National Guard unit was inducted into federal service and arrived at Camp Blanding Feb. 24, 1941, and assigned to IV Army Corps. It was transferred to Camp Shelby, MS, March 27, 1942. It was redesignated Aug 30, 1943, as HHB, IX Corps Artillery.

141ST FIELD ARTILLERY GROUP (MOTORIZED)

The 141st Field Artillery Regiment (155 mm Howitzer), a unit of the Louisiana National Guard, arrived at Camp Blanding Oct. 15, 1942. It was redesignated March 7, 1943, as HHB, 141st Field Artillery Group. Its First and Second Battalions were redesignated as 934th and 935th Field Artillery Battalions. It left Camp Blanding April 19, 1943, for the Tennessee Maneuver area, and became the 141st Field Artillery Brigade August 31, 1943.

166TH FIELD ARTILLERY GROUP (MOTORIZED)

The 166th Field Artillery Regiment (155 mm Howitzer) of the Pennsylvania National Guard arrived at Camp Blanding Oct. 15, 1942, the same day as the 141st. It followed the same redesignations, becoming HHB, 166th Field Artillery Group March 7, 1943. Its 1st Battalion was redesignated as 938th Field Artillery Battalion and its Second Battalion as 939th Field Artillery Battalion. The Group moved to Camp Gordon, GA, March 18, 1943.

17TH FIELD ARTILLERY REGIMENT (155 MM HOW)

This unit arrived at Camp Blanding March 29, 1942, and its 2nd Battalion was activated. After its training at Camp Blanding, this unit moved to the New York Port of Embarkation August 5, 1942. It served in England, North Africa and Italy.

35TH FIELD ARTILLERY REGIMENT (155 MM GUN) (MOTORIZED)

This unit was activated at Camp Blanding Feb. 10, 1941, and assigned to the 74th FA Brigade (see above). With its parent unit it was transferred to Camp Shelby, MS, March 27, 1942.

179TH FIELD ARTILLERY REGIMENT (155 MM HOW)

This Georgia National Guard unit arrived at Camp Blanding March 3, 1941, assigned to IV Army Corps. It was transferred to Camp Shelby, MS, March 23, 1943 and redesignated as 179th FA Group.

932ND FIELD ARTILLERY BATTALION (8-INCH HOW, TRACTOR)
934TH FIELD ARTILLERY BATTALION (155 MM HOW, TRUCK)
935TH FIELD ARTILLERY BATTALION (4.5-INCH GUN, TRACTOR)
938TH FIELD ARTILLERY BATTALION (155 MM HOW, TRACTOR)
939TH FIELD ARTILLERY BATTALION (4.5-INCH GUN, TRACTOR)

All of the above non-divisional field artillery battalions were activated at Camp Blanding in February and March 1943. After training at Camp Blanding, all served in the European Theater beginning in September 1943.

20TH ENGINEER COMBAT REGIMENT

This unit came to Camp Blanding from Fort Benning Jan. 15, 1942, and moved to Camp Kilmer, NJ, July 26, 1942.

A Camp Blanding company street of hutments.

AFRICAN AMERICAN TROOPS
AT CAMP BLANDING

Like most of America, the United States Army continued to follow a policy of segregation during World War II with African American troop units designated as "Colored" but with white officers. The term "Colored" was regarded in those years as the courteous way to refer to African Americans. Two African American engineer units were stationed at Camp Blanding before deployment overseas. They were trained by their own officers just as the white troops of the combat divisions had been. They were served by separate post exchange and other facilities. They were given medical care, however, at the Camp Blanding Station Hospital.

The largest of these units was the 45th Engineer General Service Regiment. It was activated at Camp Blanding on July 15, 1941. Like many other units, its Table of Organization was modified in early 1942 to authorize strength of forty-seven officers, one warrant officer and 1,150 enlisted men. It remained at that approximate strength throughout the war.

The 45th left Camp Blanding May 26, 1942, by rail and motor for the Charleston, SC, Port of Embarkation and immediate departure to Africa and subsequently to India in July. When the regiment departed Camp Blanding in 1942, its commanding officer was Colonel John C. Arrowsmith who was subsequently promoted to brigadier general the following year.

The 45th spent almost all its overseas time working on the Ledo Road, a vital supply line to General Joseph W. Stillwell's American and Chinese troops. The road from Ledo to northern Burma went through the rugged Patkai Mountains. The *Military Engineer* magazine described this unit this way: "These men work round-the-clock schedules, knee-deep in mud and harassed by insects and oppressive heat, but always manage to keep one jump ahead of Mother Nature." In this way, the 45th lived up to the high standards of service rendered by the other units which trained at Camp Blanding.

The 97th Engineer Battalion (Separate)(Colored) was activated at Camp Blanding June 1, 1941 and trained there until February 22, 1942 when it was transferred to Eglin Field, FL, and redesignated as the 97th Engineer General Service Regiment (Colored). Soon thereafter it deployed to Alaska where it constructed part of the Alaskan-Canadian Highway.

After its service in Alaska the 97th returned to Camp Sutton, N.C., and deployed again to Milne Bay, New Guinea April 24, 1944. It later served also in the Philippines. After the war's end, it was redesignated the 97th Engineer General Service Battalion (Colored) on June 30, 1946.

The 57th Ordnance Company (Colored) also was stationed at Camp Blanding but detailed service records were not available.

In addition to African American troop units on the post, a large number of African American soldiers of the Camp Blanding Station Complement designated as Headquarters Detachment No. 2 performed many duties throughout the post. This detachment is discussed in the chapter on the Station Complement. The 57th Ordnance Company also was stationed at Camp Blanding. The Camp Blanding Military Police also included a complement of Colored troops designated as Detachment No. 2, discussed in the chapter on the Military Police.

Sidney Williams of Starke, who was inducted at Camp Blanding, recalls that troops from other parts of the country encountered the strict segregation of the South for the first time but accepted it as a reality.

Retired Army Colonel Gabriel Lazar recalls his experience as a lieutenant when he was designated to escort two busloads of Colored troops from Tallahassee to Camp Blanding. They carried their lunch with them and stopped at a roadside diner to buy soft drinks for the troops and allow them to use a rest room. The proprietor refused to allow them to use the men's room and also refused to sell them soft drinks. Lt. Lazar then bought about ninety soft drinks for his troops. The white bus drivers refused to help him carry the drinks to the men. Lt. Lazar then carried them to the troops himself.

Many historians have noted that their experiences in World War II broadened the outlook of millions of Americans of all races and creeds and contributed to eventual extension of civil rights to all.

Inspection of World War II troops and their rifles at Camp Blanding.

PRISONER OF WAR CAMP

From September 1942 to April 1946 the army operated a Prisoner of War camp at Camp Blanding with such a low profile the public had scant knowledge of its size or even of its existence. It was generally ignored by local newspapers except on those rare occasions when a prisoner escaped.

Even before the Prisoner of War camp was established a group of enemy aliens who had been interned in Latin American countries were brought to Camp Blanding for temporary housing until they could be transported to permanent internment quarters in other states. They slept in pyramidal tents confined in a stockade 110 by 150 yards in area. They were supervised by a thirty-man detachment of military police. This was a new experience for all and not a pleasant one for internees or military police. Fortunately, they were at Camp Blanding only a short while during the summer of 1942 before they were transferred. Internment of civilians was unrelated to establishment of the Prisoner of War camp which was constructed a mile away from the civilian compound.

Camp Blanding was an ideal choice for the POW camp because of its mammoth size and the moderate climate. The prison compound was relatively isolated at a great distance from boundaries of the post, making escape extremely difficult. The army was concerned that civilians might be apprehensive of escaped Nazis roaming their neighborhoods. Occasional attempts to escape were inevitable, especially later when prisoners were used to harvest crops off the post, but almost all were recaptured in a few days. One nearly froze to death hiding in a refrigerator car en route to Jacksonville; another committed suicide two days after his escape. He was despondent because he had never received any mail from home while others got many letters.

An amusing incident of an escape later in the war is recalled by Captain Leon S. Theil, Camp Blanding public relations officer from March 1943 to November 1945. When the prisoner was captured, he was asked what he had lived on during his days in the woods between Camp Blanding and Jacksonville. His answer was reported in the newspapers as berries and "field mice," causing a lot of talk about a resourceful Nazi superman. On further questioning, he repeated his answer as "feldmais"—field maize or corn.

National policy toward prisoners of war was one of strict adherence to all provisions of the Geneva Convention. The United States Government feared that any mistreatment of German prisoners of war or any perception of mistreatment would result in worse retaliation against American prisoners in Europe.

Another serious concern at Camp Blanding was the conflict among prisoners themselves between those fiercely loyal to the Hitler regime and those who arrived later with a defeatist attitude.

The Camp Blanding Prisoner of War camp was activated September 24, 1942 as a German naval prison. On that date fourteen German U-Boat prisoners arrived. The Camp

Blanding navy compound was one of four in the United States. It had a capacity of 200. Additional German navy prisoners arrived including some from the pocket battleship Graf Spee, which had been sunk off the South American coast. This brought the total of prisoners to 216.

A separate compound for German army prisoners was constructed a half mile from the navy group. The first army prisoners arrived November 5, 1943. The army compound had a capacity of 1,000, but Camp Blanding was responsible for more than 4,000 prisoners of war including about 3,000 held at various times in eleven branch camps throughout Florida.

The prisoners were housed in sixteen-by sixteen-foot hutments. Mess halls were similar to those that members of the Civilian Conservation Corps had used. Each compound was surrounded by two fences with three-strand overhangs of barbed wire. Sod was removed from the area between the fences, replaced with sand and rolled to provide a "skinned" area. The army compound had eight guard towers, sited six feet above the fence line and equipped with flood lights and catwalks around the perimeter. The navy compound had four guard towers with their bases two feet above the fence line and with flood lights but no catwalks. Machine guns were mounted on the catwalks of the army compound.

The first prisoners at Blanding were survivors of German submarines. Their rabid loyalty led to beatings and death threats to newcomers they considered unpatriotic. The most serious disruptive event at the camp came when dissidents staged a strike November 15, 1943, then on December 22 staged what was termed a "riot" causing anti-Nazi prisoners to flee to protective custody of prison guards. Some of these men were transferred to another camp for their own safety. In February 1944 the situation was reversed when twenty-four German naval officers asked for transfer to another camp because they said their fellow prisoners at Camp Blanding had acquired an anti-Nazi reputation. They feared reprisals against their families in Germany because of "guilt by association."

Military Police Captain Edward C. Shannahan, representing the Provost Marshal General's Office, visited the Camp Blanding Prisoner of War camp in December 1943 and reported "The camp presents a very pleasing appearance with the buildings painted an olive drab and many pine trees growing throughout the compound area."

Captain Shannahan found medical attention to prisoners satisfactory. A prisoner of war hospital ward was maintained as part of the Camp Blanding station hospital. Sick call was held by a medical officer assigned to care for the medical needs of the prisoners. An average of twenty-five men reported for sick call each day. Overall, Captain Shannahan found only minor deficiencies although conditions in the army compound were described as "unsettled" principally because of the attitude of the spokesman for the army prisoners. He was described as "an agitator and non-conformist." He was removed. Captain Shannahan reported that none of the complaints "had any basis in fact."

The Prisoner of War camp headquarters detachment at that time consisted of six officers and twenty-seven enlisted men. It was part of the Camp Blanding station complement. Two Military Police Escort Guard Companies, the 315th and 575th MPEG Companies, were assigned to the camp.

With 1,200 young men in the two prison compounds, it was necessary to find useful work for them. They maintained their own housing and other facilities but this was not enough to keep them occupied. The Geneva Convention prohibited use of prisoners in war-related work or unusually hazardous tasks. Paul V. McNutt, chairman of the War Manpower Commission, on January 6, 1944, certified to the War Department the need for seven additional branch camps in Florida, under the supervision of the Camp Blanding POW camp commander, "in order to supply muchly needed labor in pulp wood cutting and gathering of naval stores." Prisoners also were used extensively to harvest crops in Florida.

This policy not only found useful work for the prisoners but also provided help for farmers and some businesses at a time of extreme shortage of manpower. It has been reported often that this system provided "cheap labor" for Florida employers. Not so. Users of prison labor were required to pay the government the going wage of private employers. The prisoners were paid eighty cents per day in coupons for use only to buy items stocked by the post exchange such as food, cigarettes, toiletries, etc. So important were the branch camps that groups of newly arrived prisoners were processed at Camp Blanding and sent immediately to the branch camps to help pick fruits and vegetables. Eventually Camp Blanding was responsible for fifteen branch camps and administering a total of 4,686 prisoners.

Use of prison labor away from Camp Blanding and occasional newspaper stories about escapes increased the level of public knowledge of prisoners of war in Florida. Captain Leon S. Theil, Camp Blanding public relations officer, in an address to the Starke Rotary Club in February 1945 explained that treatment of German prisoners of war was based on "twin policies of protecting Americans in German hands and easing our own manpower shortage under the Geneva Convention."

The United States Government realized more than $25,000,000 from the labor of POWs. Captain Theil said in Florida alone the government received $777,058.81 for POW contract labor in the last four months of 1944.

Congressman Bob Sikes of Florida conducted an investigation and held hearings on charges of "coddling" the prisoners. One of the frequent complaints was that prisoners' menus at Camp Blanding included culinary delicacies not enjoyed by our own troops. Investigation revealed that the culinary talent of the German cooks lay more in devising the printed menu than in preparing the food. The camp commander ordered the exotic phrases removed from the menus.

Congressman Sikes also urged the army to conduct a thorough indoctrination program to teach prisoners the workings of democracy. The Geneva Convention prohibited forcible indoctrination but Congressman Sikes said we should do it anyway "because the United States is the only country to observe the convention." In fact, the army did have a program managed in each POW camp by an Assistant Executive Officer who organized recreational programs, procured books, magazines and movies, including newsreels showing German concentration camps as Allied armies found them. After one of these concentration camp newsreels, German prisoners at Camp Blanding took up a collection for the survivors. In a note the POW spokesman said they "decided to forward the amount of $411 to the German Red Cross, to be used for women, children and men, regardless of religion, who have suffered the most during the years of the German (Nazi) government."

Generally well behaved, the German prisoners pursued their own hobbies in their spare time. Many made wood-carvings. One prisoner made a working clock using only tin cans as his materials. The Camp Blanding Museum collection includes a foot-locker fabricated by a Prisoner of War at Camp Blanding.

An insight into life in the POW camp at Camp Blanding during its final year is seen in letters home written by Richard W. Stark of Dalton, Pennsylvania. He was assigned to the military police at the POW camp from April 1945 to its closing in April 1946. On his first day he wrote, "The POWs seem to be content, and most can speak and understand English."

On May 12, 1945, he wrote home "When the news of Germany's surrender came, we manned all the towers, doubled the guard and called all of the POWs out on their company street facing the compound fence toward our quarters across the road. Then on the loud speaker the news was given to them. Some of the POWs wept but most were subdued in their response. I am sure they saw it coming."

Later Stark was assigned as a guard at the station hospital ward used only for German prisoners. He had to accompany prisoners who went for special treatment or an operation. A German doctor and a United States doctor were in charge of the ward. Three or four POW medics helped out. He wrote, "I like working at the hospital."

Starting in November 1945, prisoners were being brought back to the Camp Blanding compound for transfer to other bases on their way back to Germany. In February Stark was promoted to Private First Class, and in March he served as guard on a ten-car train of POWs to Camp Forest, Tenn. By then the prisoners were being moved out rapidly, and on April 5, 1946, only 200 were left in camp.

With some nostalgia he wrote on April 20, 1946, "It sure seems or feels lonesome here. There is only about fifty of us G.I.s here now. We cleaned the compound yesterday and nailed everything up. Today we cleaned our own area and nailed up the huts that are not being used. Tomorrow we transfer to Fort Jackson, S.C."

Richard Stark provided the drawing of the layout of the entire POW camp reproduced at page 162.

Whatever controversy existed concerning treatment of German prisoners and indoctrinating them in democracy, the prisoners have spoken often and favorably about their treatment and about America itself. Former Camp Blanding POW Paul Kurowsky visited Florida with his son in 1986. He said , "Since the end of the war, I have been pro-American. I was proud to be the first democratic man in my hometown....The others there never had the same opportunities that I experienced as a POW in America....My son didn't believe how great America is and I told him he must take a look for himself."

In the fifty years since World War II, many former prisoners of war have re-visited Camp Blanding. Most have been interviewed by James Bloodworth, first president of the Camp Blanding Museum and Historical Association. He found their comments without exception positive on their treatment and positive on what they learned about life in the United States.

This photo shows what a World War II hutment looked like from the outside with its occupants and a few guests posed at the entrance.

STATION COMPLEMENT

Camp Blanding of World War II was often referred to as the "fourth largest city of Florida." Commanding Camp Blanding and managing the large support operations was a mammoth task. It was not unlike the management of a city of comparable size, but the camp commander had responsibilities far beyond those of the mayor of a city.

To open the camp in September 1940, Major R. R. Raymond, a field artillery officer, was designated as camp commander. He signed the order activating Camp Blanding on September 14, 1940. His headquarters included one field artillery battery with three officers, one medical officer and detachments consisting of a quartermaster platoon with one officer, a staff sergeant, six clerks and two enlisted medics with one ambulance.

When the first divisions arrived for training, the senior general officer became the camp commander but detailed management of the post was left to an executive officer. The War Department soon issued an order making command of the post a separate duty of the United States Army Service

Forces headed by General Brehon B. Somervell. Within the Army Service Forces, Camp Blanding's next level of command was the Fourth Service Command in Atlanta. The divisions training at Camp Blanding were part of Army Ground Forces. When they departed, their area and facilities were taken over by the Infantry Replacement Training Center which was part of the Army Replacement and School Command.

The Army Service Forces through the camp commander provided the housing and supply needs of the huge encampment, leaving the tactical units free to devote their entire effort to their training mission. The post was responsible for receipt and issue of supplies of every kind, operation of dining facilities, maintenance of buildings, roads and vehicles—in general, for all types of logistical support except that which was the responsibility of the divisions on the post or later of the Infantry Replacement Training Center.

As early as March 12, 1941, a published Roster of Station Complement Officers listed three colonels, seven lieutenant colonels, seventeen majors, forty-five captains, sixty-seven first lieutenants, eighteen second lieutenants and one warrant officer—a total of 158. It grew much larger as the scope of activities increased.

To fulfill its responsibilities the Camp Blanding commander's headquarters included a normal army staff organization with personnel, intelligence, operations and supply divisions along with required special staff for support activities. The logistical activities included major operations with offices and warehouses as required by quartermaster, engineer, ordnance, transportation and signal elements and a purchasing agency as well as the Morale and Welfare, Public Relations and Chaplains Corps. Although War Department policy treated Public Relations as a staff position, the Public Relations Officer at Camp Blanding was assigned to the Internal Security Division with PR as an "additional duty." In three years he had no security duties.

An idea of the scope of these operations is seen in the fact that Camp Blanding employed about 4,000 civilians at the height of its role in World War II. Many civilians were housed in seven dormitories. Others commuted from Starke, Green Cove Springs, Jacksonville and Gainesville. So many military and civilian personnel lived off post that the line of cars incoming each morning and outgoing at night required more than an hour to clear the two gates.

The Camp Blanding headquarters included a separate element of African American troops in Headquarters Detachment No. 2 established in January 1941. Four years later twelve of its original members were still in the detachment. The post newspaper *Camp Blanding Report* commented that this detachment "has performed just about every job in the category of station complement functions. In 1941 it built, and for many months maintained, the railroad connecting Camp Blanding with Starke. Its members have since operated the fire department in camp, performed duties at the station hospital, Camp Headquarters, at the theaters, service clubs, the ranges and the Post Motor Pool" and "the outfit as a whole and individual members have been cited for extraordinary performance of duty."

The Camp Blanding bakery, referred to by the Quartermaster as a "T" type bakery, coke-heated, produced 25,000 pounds of bread daily at a cost of four cents per loaf. This amounted to 130,000,000 loaves of bread in its first three years of existence from 1941 to 1944. The bakery was manned by 16 enlisted men and 40 prisoners of war on two shifts. They received the raw materials, flour and yeast, from the Quartermaster and processed into bread said to be the best that could be produced at that time.

The station complement suffered frequent losses of its officers because of the urgent need for young officers in combat units. Some sad stories resulted. A new Second Lt. Al Scardiglia, just graduated from Officer Candidate School, was assigned to the station complement as liaison with the IRTC. He married the post training officer's daughter, got orders overseas immediately after the honeymoon and was killed on his first day in combat. His wife was pregnant.

Like any other city Camp Blanding had a police and fire department. It also was responsible for telephone and telegraph service initially (later contracted to Southern Bell), a water supply system, sewage disposal plants, numerous warehouses and a complete railroad system including roundhouses. The "city" also included a huge artillery range, a training area for close order drill and small unit formation drills, two infantry firing ranges, obstacle courses, modern tactical training courses and a large general maneuvers area.

Telephone service on the post began in September 1940, with seven men stringing wires on trees connecting to the Starke Telephone Company. The Bell Telephone Company took over the phone operations on the post January 16, 1943 and rapidly expanded it to an elaborate system serving the entire post. Throughout the war Southern Bell was advertising its need for more telephone operators. That was before the day of dial phones, and operators had to place every call manually. Soldiers made many long-distance calls from Camp Blanding to their homes.

Two examples of vital support operations performed at Camp Blanding involved maintenance projects in 1944. Meeting a rush order to overhaul and ship 140 two and one-half ton trucks for combat service, 200 civilians of the Combined Maintenance Shops performed this task in a ten-day spurt of activity in July 1944.

In the same month the Transportation Corps railroad roundhouse crew completely overhauled a 90-ton locomotive which operated on the post connecting Camp Blanding to the Seaboard railroad. They took the locomotive apart, cleaned its parts and replaced parts as needed. Machinists of the Combined Maintenance Shops prepared some of the required replacement parts. This entire task was performed in two weeks.

The Quartermaster Corps at Camp Blanding issued shoes in 144 different sizes ranging from 3-AAAA to size 16½ -C. Supply records showed Southern men were apt to have larger feet than men from the north. Had they gone barefoot as boys?

In August 1944 Camp Blanding received word that its civilian employees had established the best Industrial Safety record of all Army Service Forces installations in the nation. That record was 2.55 accidents per million working hours.

When the war in Europe ended, the return of troops to the states for planned redeployment to the Pacific became a priority mission. The army established a War Department Personnel Center at Camp Blanding to process these personnel, grant leaves to those to be redeployed and discharge Floridians who would not be needed for the war in the Pacific. So important was this activity that the camp commander, Brig Gen. Robert S. Israel, Jr., at that time, assumed command of the Personnel Center as well as of the camp.

Descriptions of the work of some of the major agencies on the post are in the following sections.

The Military Police Detachment at Camp Blanding maintained this motorcycle patrol during World War II.

TROOP SUPPORT

Just as the nation supported the war effort, so did military and civilian agencies and the people of the area support the World War II troops at Camp Blanding. The station complement dedicated itself to making life as pleasant as possible for military personnel, and civilian communities did likewise.

As fast as facilities could be constructed, Camp Blanding provided thirty-four branch post exchanges in addition to the main exchange with garage and photographic studio concessions and branches on sub-posts in neighboring communities. The post included eight army theaters plus an outdoor theater, five service clubs and many other facilities.

Four guesthouses and two annexes were operated to accommodate wives and relatives visiting service members. These facilities served 30,000 visitors in the year 1944.

The Red Cross played major roles in support of troops at Camp Blanding in addition to its operations at the station hospital. In October 1944 the Red Cross made its 10,000th emergency loan to a soldier at Camp Blanding. The Red Cross received about 6,500 telegrams per month concerning emergency problems of soldiers and made loans wherever needed. These interest-free loans averaged about eighty dollars each.

Three other station complement agencies assisted soldiers with personal problems. The Personal Affairs Branch assisted in matters pertaining to Emergency Maternity and Infant Care, Liaison with Office of Price Administration (to prevent over-charging by landlords or taxicabs), Death Gratuities, Allowances and Allotments and the Army Emergency Relief fund. The post Judge Advocate served as Camp Legal Assistance Officer, collaborating with the Infantry Replacement Training Center Staff Judge Advocate in cases involving IRTC personnel. The post Chaplain and twenty-four other chaplains were on call twenty-four hours per day to help any soldier solve an immediate personal problem.

Troops using the recreational facilities of Kingsley Lake could count on the Transportation Corps for life-saving service. Nine lives were saved in the summer of 1943 and fifteen lives were saved in the summer of 1944 on Kingsley Lake by the Transportation Corps speedboat life-saving team.

Other government agencies also served soldiers on Camp Blanding. By early 1944 the post office had opened five branch outlets in addition to the main post office. The branches were open from noon to 9:30 p.m. six days per week, and the main post office was open on Sundays as well as weekdays.

Internal Revenue Service came to Camp Blanding to assist all soldiers with income tax filing. Agents set up a schedule with days allotted to serve troops of the Infantry Replacement Training Center, Station Complement and hospital patients, each in their own areas of the post.

Evening entertainment on the post was provided throughout the war by a host of stars of the time including Major Bowes' Amateur Hour, Harpo Marx, Alec Templeton, Phil

Spitalny, Rubinoff and Jose Iturbi. Two of the biggest occasions were dances with music by Jack Teagarden in November 1944 and Sammy Kaye in March 1945. Participants filled the Field House on both occasions, and both were broadcast nationally on network radio.

Free long distance telephone calls for hospital patients at Christmas 1944 were provided as a gift from the American Legion Post No. 9 of Jacksonville. For patients who could not be moved, telephones were installed in their wards and calls made directly from their beds.

Merchants and civic associations in nearby communities offered facilities to help serve military needs. Jacksonville department stores provided window display space for exhibits promoting nurse and WAC recruitment.

Citizens of Starke and Keystone Heights in 1945 offered free homesite lots to any service member who agreed to build a home there as soon as materials became available. This reflected the friendly attitude toward soldiers at Camp Blanding shown by the surrounding civilian communities generally throughout the war.

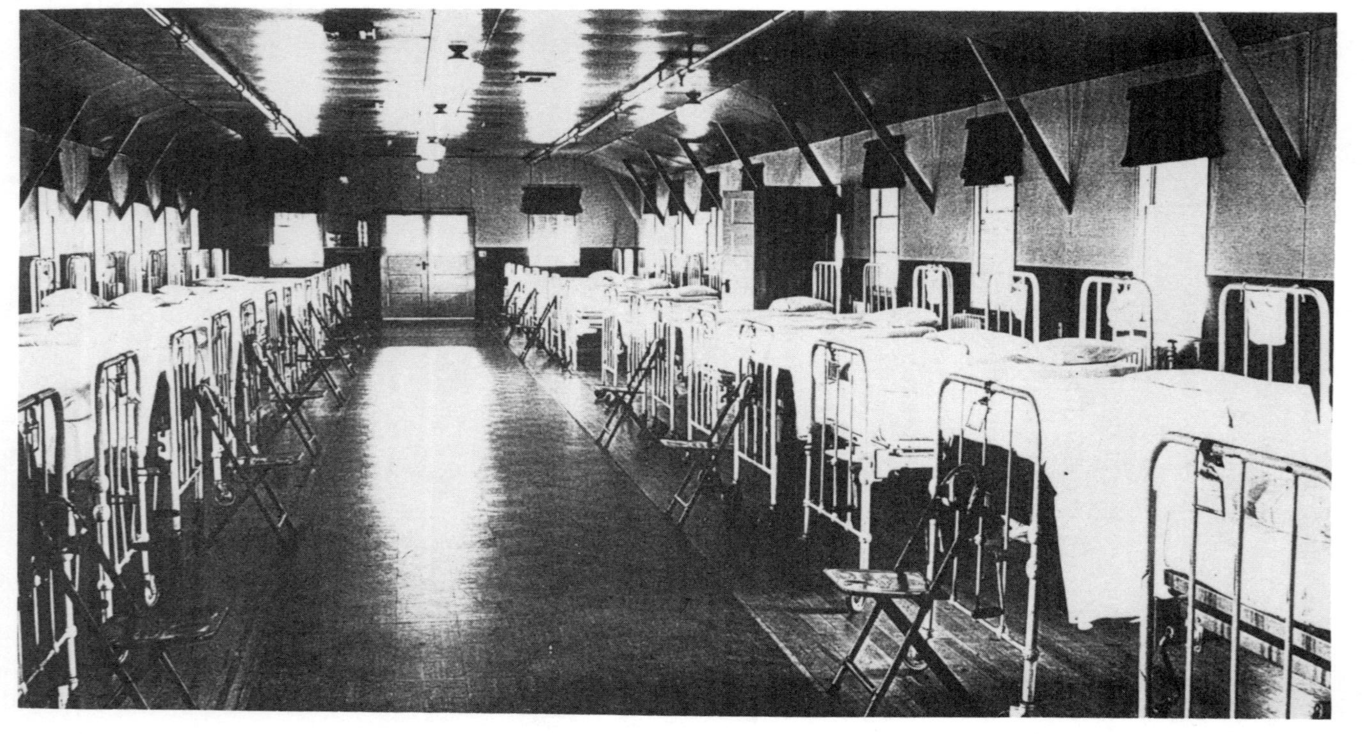

This typical surgical ward in the Camp Blanding Station hospital was known as a W-1 type. It was building B-8 in 1943.

RELIGIOUS SERVICES

World War II troops at Camp Blanding were served by a corps of chaplains usually numbering twenty-eight providing religious services at twenty-four chapels throughout the post. All chapels were constructed in a manner to accommodate services of any denomination. Throughout the war chaplains of the Catholic, Protestant and Jewish faiths were always on duty at Camp Blanding. An editorial in the May 17, 1944, issue of the post newspaper, *The Camp Blanding Report*, noted that the post chaplains "keep twenty-four chapels and one theater well filled with from one to a half dozen services apiece on Sunday mornings and at other appropriate occasions—67,000 men attended 575 services last month."

On D-Day in June 1944 devotional services were held in twelve chapels with total attendance of 1,000 worshippers. At the post chapel forty-five members of the WAC detachment were present along with civilians and other military personnel. In his weekly column in the post newspaper Chaplain Edwin R. Carter, the post Chaplain wrote, "the service was most impressive with many prayers said by members of the congregation."

On V-E Day services were held in the evening at all post chapels, and on the following Sunday a memorial was held at all regular services in accord with President Truman's proclamation of May 13, 1945 as a day of prayer.

In April 1944 Chaplain Ernest R. Armstrong started a class in elementary reading and writing. Chaplain Carter explained in his post newspaper column that the main purpose of these classes was "to make it possible for all colored troops in the station complement to read the Bible and notices on the bulletin boards as well as to be able to write to the folks at home."

The chaplains at Camp Blanding made themselves available to soldiers twenty-four hours per day for individual counseling and any assistance they could render. The chaplains were adaptable to the religious preferences of soldiers. For example, after attending a sermon in September 1945, two soldiers expressed a desire to be baptized by immersion. The chaplain arranged and conducted a service with baptism by immersion in Kingsley Lake.

The Corps of Chaplains was one of the four agencies on the post coordinating their efforts to provide all needed personal services to the troops.

MILITARY POLICE

The Security and Intelligence Division at Camp Blanding was responsible for Military Police matters in an area comprising more than half the state of Florida for most of World War II. Camp Blanding was by far the largest army post in Florida with responsibility for many sub-posts and branch prisoner of war camps.

Headed by Lt. Col. S.E. Minikes as Director of the S and I Division, the force included eight officers and 350 enlisted men. As the "fourth largest city in Florida," Camp Blanding itself was a major responsibility of the Military Police. Traffic control, investigating and testifying at courts martial, guarding prisoners, finding missing children and dealing with emergencies during the dark hours of the night were routine MP duties.

In addition, the Camp Blanding MPs were behind many of the arrests finally made by civilian federal agencies such as narcotics agents, Treasury Department agents, postal inspectors and the FBI. To cover the thirty-two counties, for which they were responsible, the Camp Blanding MP Detachment maintained district offices in St. Augustine, Palatka, Ocala and Gainesville.

An important element of the MP Detachment on the post was a group of thirty-seven civilians who joined the force April 10, 1944 as a civilian auxiliary to release some soldiers for other duty. Many of these recruits were World War I veterans. All were given intensive police training by Major Lloyd H. Lewis, Chief of the Security Branch of the detachment. From the inception of the auxiliary, these men wore the regulation army uniform with a special "Auxiliary Police" shoulder patch. Upon completion of their training they were given full police authority over both civilians and military on the post.

Throughout the war a separate element of the Military Police on the post was MP Section Two, a detachment of African American troops activated in April 1942 with a strength of thirty-seven enlisted men. Before the end of 1943 it had grown to a strength of 118. On the post the Ordnance Service Command Shops, Post Motor Pool, Camp Finance Office, Warehouse area, Bank and Camp Headquarters building were under guard by this detachment. In addition to traffic control in D Area of the post, this group patrolled in Starke, Gainesville and Jacksonville.

Effectiveness of the Military Police force at Camp Blanding can be inferred from the low rate of both major and minor crimes.

FIRE DEPARTMENT

The civilian-operated fire department at Camp Blanding gave credit to the troops on the post for the remarkable record of negligible fire loss throughout World War II.

Fire protection was necessary from the beginning of the post. The contractors, who built the post, Starrett Brothers and Eken, established the first fire department October 17, 1940. It consisted of four pick-up trucks and a group of civilians who could man fire extinguishers when necessary. The army took over this responsibility the next month. A motorized Ford 500-gallon pumper arrived, and soon Fire Chief L. C. Moore had twenty-five civilian firefighters. The department grew as the camp grew. It acquired ten modern fire trucks including two 750-gallon pumpers and eight 500-gallon pumpers.

Success of the fire department is measured in the fact that fire loss on the post was less than one cent per year per man on the post. Fire Chief W. W. Letts said, "We have never had a hutment burn to the ground and have never lost a major building." He gave credit to the troops, saying, "the soldiers of this post deserve the entire credit for the success we have achieved.... Soldiers practice fire prevention effectively and are definitely fire conscious."

The Military Police Detachment at Camp Blanding had this baseball team for intra-mural competition.

WACs AT CAMP BLANDING

More than 500 female soldiers, members of the Women's Army Corps, made a record during World War II at Camp Blanding that helped establish the future role of women in the military. They filled thirty-seven different jobs from accountant to X-ray technician and won commendations from the senior commanders throughout the post.

The officer and enlisted cadre arrived May 24, 1943, to prepare for activation of the detachment, first known as Women's Auxiliary Army Corps (WAAC). The officers were Second Officer Elizabeth H. Branch and Third Officer Margaret K. Ellis. They were not called lieutenants in the WAAC. The enlisted cadre of eleven members was led by First Leader Una M. Bourgeois who later became First Sergeant.

The detachment was activated June 1, 1943. On August 14, 1943, eighty-three women were sworn in, and on August 23, ten more were sworn in. On September 1, 1943, the detachment was redesignated the Women's Army Corps Detachment No. 1, and ranks became the same as in the rest of the army. The detachment strength quickly rose to 110 and remained at or above that level. Its peak strength was 258. There was a constant flow of transfers to other assignments including many deployed overseas. In addition to assignments in the detachment, WAC officers filled important executive positions on the post in Signal Office, Finance, Hospital, Special Services, Quartermaster and Induction Station.

When the first female soldiers arrived, they found their area not quite ready for them. They adapted quickly, setting up their own beds in their two barracks. They ate temporarily in the hospital mess hall. For the first two weeks they were restricted to their area but thereafter were given freedom of movement within the camp. Transition from civilian to military life was not without incident for the WACs. A new WAC lieutenant, fresh from her career as a New York department store buyer, was taken on an orientation tour of the post. She observed men eating from mess kits beside the road and observed "How nice—a picnic." The Regular Army driver nearly lost control of the jeep.

To whatever extent the traditional male objection to women in the army existed at Camp Blanding, these women overcame the prejudice. The new WAC Detachment quickly established itself as a significant unit in the operations of Camp Blanding. Before it was one-year-old, Fourth Service Command in Atlanta had recognized the unit as one of its two best WAC detachments. Commendations for their performance of duty on jobs throughout the post were common. They participated generously in War Bond drives and Red Cross fund-raising, gave blood transfusions and marched in an Armistice Day parade in Jacksonville. A photograph in the post newspaper showed them marching smartly in step. The WAC correspondent wrote in the newspaper about this event that "The applause the detachment received as it marched through the streets of Jacksonville on Armistice Day was thrilling and morale-building, as well as assurance that the citizenry approved and admired their efforts."

In a time of shortages of workers, WACs helped out with part-time jobs in their off hours on the post. At one time twenty WACs worked at night in fourteen different post exchanges. Lt. Andrew Sweet, the post exchange officer, said they were "very, very efficient, their discipline and character are beyond reproach, and they are always well-groomed and attractive (and) there have been no cases of friction between civilians and WACs." Other WACs did similar off-duty work at the camp theaters.

Morale must have been high among the WACs. When their time for drill was changed from the heat of Friday afternoons to Wednesday and Thursday mornings from 6:15AM to 6:30AM, their correspondent wrote in the post newspaper that most of the members "feel this is a welcome change."

The WAC social calendar was always a full one. The first big event was a dance on August 13, 1943, given by the camp commander, Brigadier General L. A. Kunzig, to celebrate the conversion of the WAAC to the WAC. Male members of the Station Complement were also guests. Dinners and dances were offered with WACs as guests on many occasions at service clubs, NCO clubs, the hospital area, the Infantry Replacement Training Center and at other military installations off post.

The WACs drew strong support from the women of Jacksonville through a WAC Recruiting Committee of the Duval County Defense Council. Fifty members of that committee made an all-day visit to the WAC detachment, inspected the facilities, had lunch with the WACs and observed a precision drill which drew prolonged applause.

When the United States Army Recreation Center was opened in St. Augustine, a section with facilities for women was included and the Camp Blanding WACs were invited to use it without cost. Many did use it frequently beginning in the summer of 1944.

At the end of their first year at Camp Blanding, the WAC detachment was honored at a retreat parade and a special dinner in the WAC mess hall following a reception in their day room with WAC songs sung by the entire group. Their first year at Camp Blanding saw fifteen WAC weddings and twenty more the second year.

The WACs acquired a pet of sorts in mid-1944 in the form of a baby chick. The WACs named her Mabel. The chick grew up and began laying an egg a day much to the pleasure of the WACs. Then Corporal Edna Robertson, WAC cook, brought three baby chicks back from town, and Mabel adopted them as her own. This was in November 1944. Alas, by January 10, 1945, the post newspaper reported that three dogs had invaded Mabel's home in the boiler room, ending the saga of Mabel and her three adopted chicks.

The WAC detachment at Camp Blanding had five commanding officers: LT. Elizabeth H. Branch, LT. Margaret K. Ellis, Capt. Phyllis M. Roos, Capt. Mary V. Racey and Capt. Josephine F. Kenny.

As long as they were needed, the WACs served at Camp Blanding. When the war ended in the Pacific, the WACs joined the processing system for discharges—or re-enlistments in some cases—in the same manner as the men.

STATION HOSPITAL

From the time the first troops arrived at Camp Blanding in September 1940, the station hospital provided medical service. The planned 2,000-bed hospital was under construction, so early sickness cases were cared for satisfactorily in mess halls temporarily used as wards with army cots serving as hospital beds.

On Christmas Eve 1940 the new hospital came into operation with one ward and one mess hall. The original hospital staff consisted of four Regular Army Medical Corps officers, one Regular Army Medical Administrative Corps officer and twenty-four Reserve Officers of the Medical Corps, Dental Corps, Medical Administrative Corps and Veterinary Corps plus four nurses for a total staff of thirty-three.

The first year of the hospital was hectic for its doctors and nurses. Some 31st Division troops arrived even before the first twenty-five bed element of hospital equipment came. Many items of this equipment were back-ordered, and the hospital bought many of its supplies on the open market that first year. The enormity of the hospital construction, manning and operation is seen in the fact that by the end of its first year (1941), the hospital consisted of 126 buildings.

When an influenza epidemic hit the post in December 1940 and January 1941, drugs were scarce. No codeine was available to alleviate the suffering of hundreds of influenza patients. The hospital bought a supply of codeine in Jacksonville, so large that the Narcotics Bureau sent a man to the post to investigate. He took one look and returned to Jacksonville.

Many other unforeseen problems were solved through the initiative of hospital personnel. The hospital conducted necessary training programs for all doctors, nurses and enlisted personnel throughout the year. In his 1941 Annual Report to the Surgeon General of the Army, the hospital commander, Col. L. R. Poust, commented that "the adaptability of the personnel to the different assignments that were new and to which they were unaccustomed has been splendid. It is believed that the entire staff has profited from experience gained from their duties."

In the same report Colonel Poust also noted that "most of these difficulties were overcome and the institution built up to a state of completion as to organization, supplies and equipment and professional facilities so that on July 2, 1941, this hospital received recognition by the American College of Surgeons."

When the hospital was built, all the native vegetation in the area was removed, leaving glaring white sand, which was hard on the eyes and added to the heat. A drafted soldier with horticultural experience was able to grow shrubbery, flowers and some vegetables on the hospital grounds with only small expenditures from the Hospital Fund. Oak, cedar, magnolia, holly, dogwood, chinaberry and palm trees were added.

The fact that many units spent part of 1941 on maneuvers in Louisiana somewhat alleviated the patient load at the hospital. However, soldiers needing hospital care were returned to Camp Blanding from the maneuver area. These returns ranged from one or two cars to a special train of thirteen coaches.

As the hospital grew in 1941, specialization in diagnosis and treatment became necessary. Sections were established for Neuropsychiatric, Gastro-Intestinal, Cardiovascular, Dermatological and Allergy cases as well as a Contagious and Infectious Section and a Medical Section for Colored troops. The Surgical Service also was organized into separate sections for General Surgery; Septic Surgery; Eye, Ear, Nose and Throat; Genito-Urinary; Physiotherapy, and Orthopedic.

Equipment for a ten-chair Dental Clinic arrived in February 1941 followed shortly by an additional four-chair unit. Laboratory Service began in the hospital in January 1941 with the assistance of the University of Florida and the Florida State Board of Health for the loan of supplies not available from army sources. The need for this help was apparent as the Laboratory averaged more than 10,000 tests and procedures per month for the nine months it was in operation. Out-patient Service was organized May 15, 1941, and quickly became a major integral part of the hospital with a total of 30,624 treatments and physical examinations in the year 1941.

One year after the hospital opened, the *Bulletin* of the Camp Blanding station hospital on Christmas Day 1941 compared the hospital then with the situation one year earlier. "It was emergency basis then, not war, and tents were a good deal more uncomfortable (with the freezing temperatures and continuous rain) than the accommodations we now enjoy. It was none too pleasant standing in chow line in a cold drizzle or running back and forth in the mud to makeshift and crowded wards." The writer then noted that "all of us, warm, well fed, comfortably housed" could enjoy a Merry Christmas.

In that first full year of operation, the hospital had 22,047 admissions, of which 19,779 cases were diseases and 2,268 were injuries. The most common disease was influenza with 3,821 admissions. At year-end 1941 the hospital had 132 male officers, 150 nurses, 331 enlisted men and 537 civilian employees.

Having commanded the hospital from its inception through its early expansion and formal organization phases, Colonel Poust ended his tenure as hospital commander April 8, 1942. He was succeeded for just one week, April 8—15, by Lt. Col. William T. Weissinger, and from April 15 to September 3 by Lt. Col. James M. Troutt who was promoted to colonel April 23, 1942. Colonel Charles B. Callard took command of the hospital September 4, 1942, and remained as commander for the rest of the war.

In his Annual Report Colonel Callard wrote that the year 1942 would be remembered "chiefly because of the many changes in the daily life of all personnel brought about by military necessity." Blackouts were strictly enforced on the post, including the hospital. Colonel Callard described the blackout problems this way:

The blackouts presented many new problems such as the type of blackout curtains to be used; whether or not to turn out the red lights on telephone poles in the hospital area indicating the presence of a fire alarm box; the problems of dispatching ambulances at night during a blackout and many others. The night ward nurses had to have lights so oil lanterns were placed in buckets and shielded. Arguments as to what color small lights might be safely used at corridor intersections wavered between red, blue and green. Nurses learned to 'make up' and officers to shave in the dark. Fortunately, no accidents or incidents of any consequence occurred in either of these activities.

Twice during 1942 broken water mains in the hospital corridors occurred at night. The combination of low temperatures, cold gushing water, total darkness and absence of trained utility personnel tested the ingenuity of the night staff at the hospital. Further expansion of the hospital was clearly needed in 1942. Troop strength on post was approximately 56,000, and the hospital was required also to serve troops in the vicinity of Jacksonville, St. Augustine, Gainesville and Starke. Under Medical Corps formulas the total requirement would be 2,420-bed capacity. The hospital solved this problem by converting four barracks to wards and adding expansion beds to many wards, reaching a bed capacity of 2,350. At December 31, 1942, the number of patients was 2,090. Colonel Callard reported to the Surgeon General of the Army that the hospital facilities were "inadequate for a camp of this size considering the number of outside personnel that have to be serviced." The required expansion would come in 1943. Within the hospital complex, the commander re-arranged many facilities to attain most efficient use of bed space. For the year 1942, hospital admissions totaled 20,823 of which 18,369 were diseases and 2,184 injuries.

On Christmas Day 1942 an attractive Christmas dinner souvenir menu included a roster of hospital personnel headed by the hospital commander, Col. Charles B. Callard, MC. It listed 137 male officers, ninety-two station hospital nurses and an additional 145 nurses assigned to other hospital units on the post. In addition, the Medical Detachment, commanded by First Lt. Harold E. Howland, listed 814 enlisted men. A separate Medical Detachment No. 2 listed 229 enlisted men. A total of 272 civilian employees were listed as well as the Mess Department consisting of 187 military personnel and thirty-six civilians. This made a total of 1,912 persons working at the hospital by the end of 1942. During the year 1943 the hospital expanded to its required 2,800-bed capacity with the addition of thirty-four new buildings and the conversion of some existing buildings to meet specific medical needs. Additional 100 beds could be made available on twenty-four hours notice by utilizing existing buildings in the labor camp area. For emergencies the post quartermaster kept in storage 500 complete sets of beds including bedding.

When the last of the major army units left Camp Blanding, an Infantry Replacement Training Center was activated August 15, 1943. This change materially increased the hospital workload. The large tactical units had their own medical personnel to provide their own medical care except for hospitalization. The IRTC did not have this capability.

For the remainder of its existence, the hospital adapted to these changed conditions. The IRTC received 5,400 new recruits every three weeks, many of whom were in poor physical condition with communicable disease potentials and visual and dental problems. The seventeen weeks of strenuous training of these recruits in the IRTC created above average hospitalization rates because of injuries (orthopedic and surgical cases) and neuropsychiatric problems.

Throughout the post the post surgeon operated medical dispensaries with personnel assigned to Camp Blanding headquarters. The need for hospitalization was determined at the dispensaries, and patients were conveyed by ambulance to the hospital newly constructed receiving building where an Admissions Officer examined patients and made ward assignments.

The hospital workload was also heavy through its assistance to the Army Examination Board. In his report to the Surgeon General of the Army, Colonel Callard noted that "one of the most important functions of the Allergy Section is elimination of allergic inductees prior to their induction." Opinions rendered by this clinic prevented the induction of men with allergies who would have become qualified for Disability Discharges within three months.

Further evidence of the increasing workload is seen in the increasing numbers of outpatients. The total number of outpatients in 1943 was 751,228. This was an impressive figure since the IRTC was in operation for less than six months of the year. The average number of outpatients grew to more than 170,000 per month.

The hospital commander found fault with the army system, which required that all individuals complete basic training before assignment to non-combat duty. Individuals with physical weaknesses often started basic training only to suffer illness or injury after a few weeks, enter the hospital, get treatment, and then return to the IRTC. The individual would then have to join a subsequent training group to start over his basic training, then repeat the process of hospitalization and further delays. This situation aggravated the shortage of medical officer, which the commander deemed "the most agonizing problem" of the station hospital. Next in order of their importance, he wrote, was the "shortage of (1) Nurses, (2) Dental Officers and (3) Medical Administrative officers."

As they had done in the first year of its operation, Hospital personnel continued to exercise initiative to solve many unexpected problems and provide the required care for personnel at Camp Blanding and military facilities in surrounding communities as well as family members of eligible personnel. In the Women's Section 178 babies were born in 1943. Recollections today of personnel who served at Camp Blanding during World War II jibe closely with existing hospital records.

Dr. Samuel Day of Jacksonville, FL, served at the hospital for three years. He recalls being assigned first to the venereal disease ward, but he pulled strings and finally was assigned to the surgery unit. He recalls the 63rd General Hospital and 6th Evacuation Hospital providing support to the station hospital through an informal arrangement while those units were at Camp Blanding.

Hospital records show that medical units assigned to temporary duty or attached to Camp Blanding, mostly with small numbers of nurses on duty, included the 6th and 37th General Hospital; 54th, 79th, 115th, 227th and 264th station hospital; 16th, 94th, and 41st Evacuation Hospital. Enlisted personnel of these and other medical units participated in training with enlisted personnel of the Camp Blanding station hospital.

Julian K. Wood, who served three years as a statistician in the hospital Registrar's Office, today recalls expansion of the hospital with four rows of twenty-one wards each. A, B, and C sections were for the bed patients. D section held mess halls, offices and supply rooms. Elsewhere on the post was a Rehabilitation Center to which patients recuperating from serious operations were transferred.

Wood also recalls use of the new drug penicillin. It was held exclusively for military patients and not available under any circumstances for non-military personnel.

WACs played an increasingly important role at the hospital. The 1944 Christmas dinner menu at the hospital showed a total of 135 members of the Hospital WAC Detachment.

The Red Cross played an important role in the hospital throughout World War II. Red Cross personnel were assigned to the hospital beginning in March 1941 with a small office on one of the wards and a recreation room at the rear of the Hospital Chapel. In January 1942 a Patients' Recreation Building for Red Cross activities was completed. It included a library with more than 2,000 books for use of patients. By 1944 the Red Cross staff at the hospital included 16 professional workers and four clerks.

In July 1944 the Camp Blanding station hospital was designated by the War Department as a Regional Station Hospital. The purpose of this designation was to take part of the load off general hospitals in the area. The Camp Blanding regional hospital then accepted military hospital cases within a seventy-five mile radius of Camp Blanding and sent to general hospitals only those cases requiring specialized treatment not available at Camp Blanding. As a Regional Station hospital, it also established an Army Retirement Board and a Retirement Board for Army Nurses. The Camp Blanding regional station hospital continued to function in this fashion until the end of the war and through the demobilization activities at Camp Blanding.

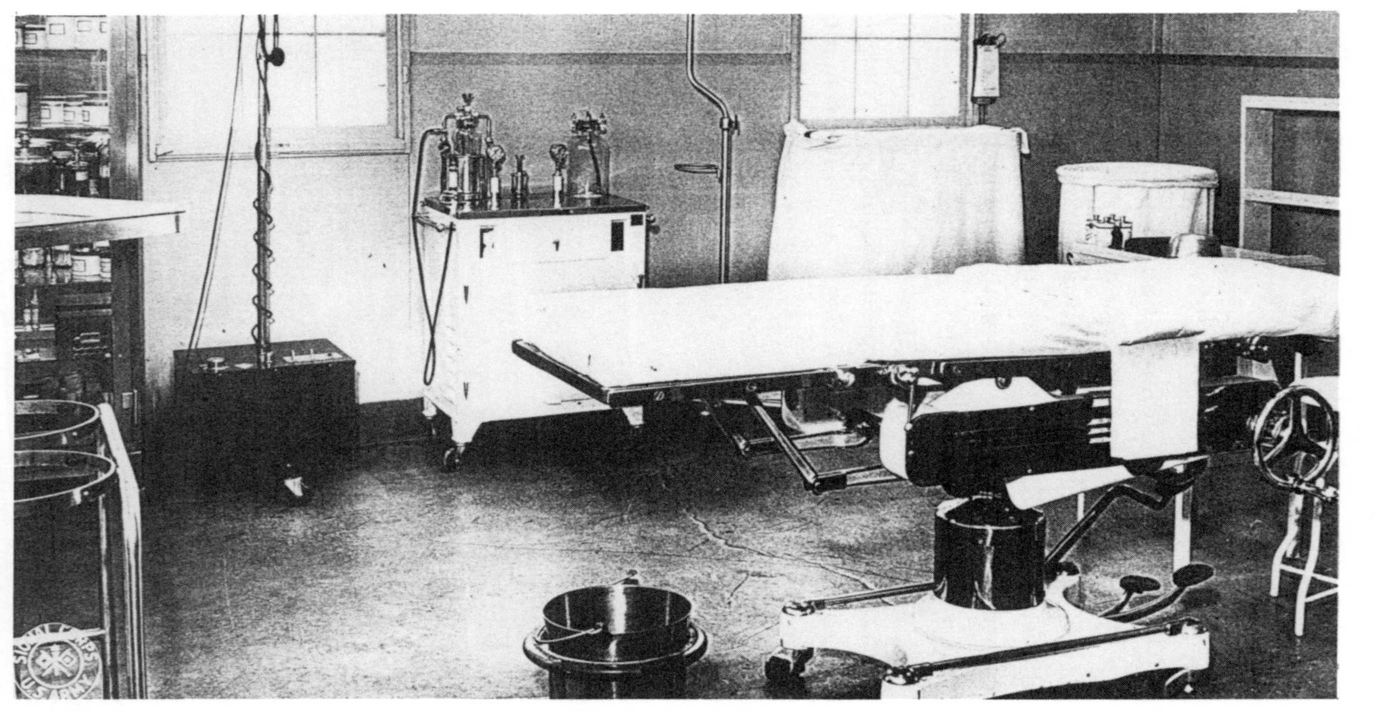

This was a typical operating room in the Camp Blanding Station hospital in 1943. This was Building A-12.

INFANTRY REPLACEMENT
TRAINING CENTER

In August 1943 the last two army divisions, the 66th and 63rd, departed from Camp Blanding, leaving housing and training facilities available for at least 30,000 troops. The Army's greatest need at that time was trained infantry soldiers as replacements for battle casualties and as fillers for understrength combat units.

The War Department moved immediately to establish an Infantry Replacement Training Center (IRTC) at Camp Blanding as soon as the two divisions departed. The IRTC as the facility to provide basic training for new recruits was well established within the army with eight other IRTCs already in operation, all in the South except Camp Roberts in southern California. The IRTCs were part of the Replacement and School Command, one of the Army's major commands. It was located in Birmingham, Alabama, and commanded by Major General Harry W. Hazlett.

Brig Gen. Eugene W. Fales, later promoted to Major General, commanded the IRTC from its inception. His Executive Officer. Lt. Col. Apablasa was known to everybody on the post. He was a strong personality, a disciplined infantry officer who fit the requirements of the IRTC to train infantrymen. His counterpart in the Station Complement was a similar personality. Lt. Col (later Colonel) Harry A. Johnston, a lawyer and reservist, was equally dedicated to accomplishment of the missions of this vast army post.

The mission of the IRTC was to provide sufficient basic training to individual infantry soldiers to qualify them for assignment to combat units upon completion of the seventeen weeks of training. The training was conducted in prescribed blocks of instruction beginning with the elementary lessons of soldiering which General Fales described as the ability to "march, shoot and salute." It then progressed to the mastery of all the individual and crew-served weapons of the infantry regiment. Each individual was then given advanced training in the tactics and weapons employment of one of the standard infantry company organizations—rifle, heavy weapons, antitank and cannon companies as well as headquarters and service companies. The final three weeks of the seventeen-week program were devoted to field training when troops went on bivouac, slept on the ground and learned to operate without the amenities of the camp itself.

Each individual trainee received a booklet titled "I Am a Doughboy" describing the mission and weapons of each unit within the infantry regiment with a notation to the individual citing the pages where the duties for which he was being trained were described.

The training program included the following elements:

Rifle Company. Rifle squad, light machine gun (.30 caliber, air-cooled) squad and 60 mm mortar squad.

Heavy Weapons Company. Heavy machine gun (.30 caliber, water-cooled) squad and 81 mm mortar squad.

Cannon Company. 105 mm howitzer, .30 caliber carbine and bazooka.

Antitank Company. 57 mm antitank platoon, .50 caliber machine gun, .30 caliber carbine and antitank mine platoon.

Headquarters Company. Intelligence and reconnaissance platoon, communications platoon, wire section, radio and visual section.

Service Company. Buglers, cooks, motor mechanics, truck drivers, clerks and stenographers, armorer-artificers and pioneers, all to be trained on the rifle, carbine and .50 caliber machine-gun.

To support the infantry-training program, a field artillery battalion was assigned to the IRTC to provide realistic overhead fire while trainees were on tactical exercises. The 464th Parachute Field Artillery Battalion provided this until the 75th Field Artillery Battalion, which returned from deployment to Alaska, replaced it in August 1944.

Upon completion of this program, the trainees were assigned to units, mostly infantry divisions preparing for early combat missions. The standardization of infantry training and combat tactics enabled soldiers trained in the IRTC to fit immediately into any army division, only needing to get acquainted with their fellow squad members and identify their specific roles within the unit.

Upon arrival at the Camp Blanding IRTC, soldiers were checked to verify they had complete uniform and individual equipment, had passed the physical examination and were ready to start the training. While undergoing basic training, soldiers were not given furloughs except in emergency verified by the Red Cross. Weekend passes to visit nearby communities could be authorized for up to twenty-five percent of a unit.

The IRTC was organized into eleven Infantry Training Regiments numbered 60 through 70. Each regiment had four Infantry Training Battalions numbered 190th through 232nd. The 63rd, 64th, 65th, 67th, and 68th Regiments occupied the area originally used by the 43rd Division. The 60th, 61st, 62nd, 66th and 69th Regiments occupied the area originally used by the 31st Division. The 70th Regiment was divided with half of its troops on each side of the old "Mason Dixon Line." The map at page 122 shows the layout of the IRTC on the post.

All post facilities for entertainment, transportation, sports participation, etc., described elsewhere in this book, were available to IRTC personnel and extensively used. IRTC teams participated in sports competitions on the post. An IRTC dance band frequently played for dances on the post, and IRTC personnel were often guests at dances arranged by the WAC detachment of the Station Complement.

The IRTC sponsored open house at Camp Blanding to commemorate Infantry Day June 15, 1944. Exhibits, demonstrations, a formal parade with an award ceremony and speech by Senator Claude Pepper drew nearly 5,000 civilian visitors and 422 visiting military personnel from other posts.

The IRTC published *The Bayonet*, a weekly newspaper for its troops with information about on-post activities and events within the IRTC. The center also produced a daily *War News Digest* posted on all company bulletin boards and urged all troops to read it as a method of keeping informed about progress of the war.

The IRTC participated actively in War Bond Drives, more than doubling its quota in the 1945 campaign with total bond purchases of $2,147,955 by IRTC personnel.

When the war ended in the Pacific, the Camp Blanding Public Relations Office estimated that between 300,000 and 400,000 soldiers had passed through its gates since activation in September 1940 of whom 175,000 had been trained at the IRTC. Because the IRTC continued to operate for some months after V-J Day to meet the continuing need for replacements, it seems clear the Camp Blanding IRTC trained at least 200,000 soldiers.

Along with its weapons and tactical training, the IRTC program sought to make its soldiers justifiably proud to be infantrymen. The "I Am a Doughboy" booklet reminded these soldiers "In combat, my primary mission is to close with the enemy and destroy or capture him. While all of the other arms and services render indispensable support, it is the action of the infantry which will bring the present war to a decisive and victorious conclusion."

Monument at Camp Blanding honoring trainees of the Infantry Replacement Training Center.

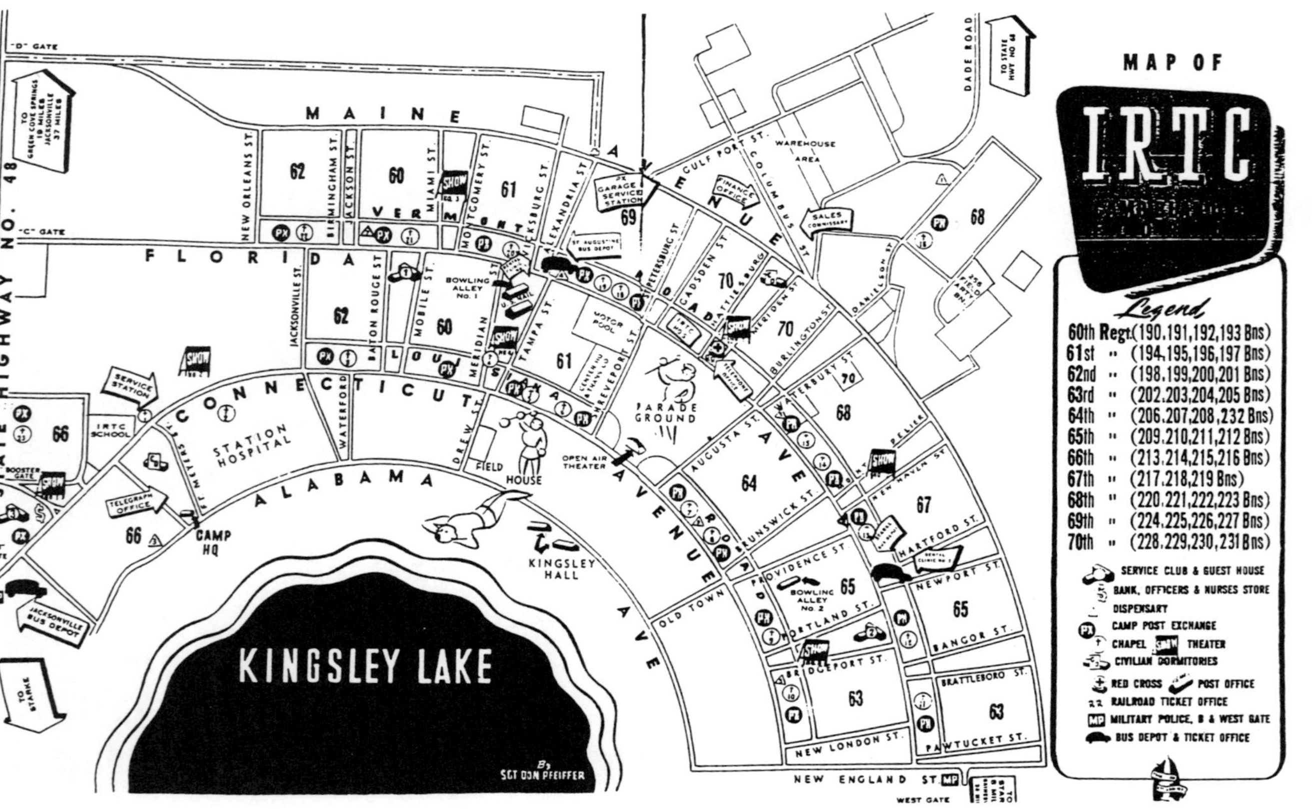

MAP OF
IRTC
Legend
60th Regt.(190,191,192,193 Bns)
61st " (194,195,196,197 Bns)
62nd " (198,199,200,201 Bns)
63rd " (202,203,204,205 Bns)
64th " (206,207,208,232 Bns)
65th " (209,210,211,212 Bns)
66th " (213,214,215,216 Bns)
67th " (217,218,219 Bns)
68th " (220,221,222,223 Bns)
69th " (224,225,226,227 Bns)
70th " (228,229,230,231 Bns)
SERVICE CLUB & GUEST HOUSE
BANK, OFFICERS & NURSES STORE
DISPENSARY
CAMP POST EXCHANGE
CHAPEL   THEATER
CIVILIAN DORMITORIES
RED CROSS   POST OFFICE
RAILROAD TICKET OFFICE
MILITARY POLICE, B & WEST GATE
BUS DEPOT & TICKET OFFICE
MAINE
VERMONT
FLORIDA
CONNECTICUT
ALABAMA
STATE HIGHWAY NO. 48
"D" GATE
"C" GATE
TO GREEN COVE SPRINGS 10 MILES JACKSONVILLE 37 MILES
TO STARKE
BOOSTER GATE
"E" GATE
NEW ORLEANS ST
BIRMINGHAM ST
JACKSON ST
MIAMI ST
MONTGOMERY ST
VICKSBURG ST
ALEXANDRIA ST
JACKSONVILLE ST
BATON ROUGE ST
MOBILE ST
MERIDIAN ST
TAMPA ST
DREW ST
FT MEYERS ST
SHREVEPORT ST
PETERSBURG ST
GADSDEN ST
GULF PORT ST
COLUMBUS ST
DANIELSON ST
BURLINGTON ST
WATERBURY AVE
AUGUSTA ST
BRUNSWICK ST
NEW HAVEN ST
HARTFORD ST
NEWPORT ST
PROVIDENCE ST
PORTLAND ST
BRIDGEPORT ST
BANGOR ST
BRATTLEBORO ST
NEW LONDON ST
PAWTUCKET ST
NEW ENGLAND ST
OLD TOWN AVE
WEST GATE
AVENUE
WATERFORD
SERVICE STATION
IRTC SCHOOL
STATION HOSPITAL
TELEGRAPH OFFICE
CAMP HQ
KINGSLEY HALL
FIELD HOUSE
OPEN AIR THEATER
PARADE GROUND
MOTOR POOL
GARAGE SERVICE STATION
FINANCE OFFICE
SALES COMMISSARY
WAREHOUSE AREA
ST. AUGUSTINE BUS DEPOT
JACKSONVILLE BUS DEPOT
BOWLING ALLEY NO. 1
BOWLING ALLEY NO. 2
KINGSLEY LAKE
By SGT DON PFEIFFER
DADE ROAD
TO STATE HWY NO 64
FIELD ARTY BNS

FLORIDA STATE GUARD

When substantially all of a state's National Guard is called to active federal service, need arises for the organization of a state armed force to meet emergencies and internal security needs. With the major call-ups in 1940, Congress enacted legislation in October 1940 specifically authorizing states to organize and maintain such state armed forces under these circumstances.

The Florida Legislature enacted a statute April 22, 1941 to provide for the creation and maintenance of "such military forces, as the governor may deem necessary to assist the civil authorities in maintaining law and order." Camp Blanding came into the picture as a major training site for these state forces.

Upon enactment of the Florida law, the Office of the Adjutant General issued the necessary regulations governing organization, equipment, maintenance, discipline, training and operation of the force. Members were not paid except when they were called to state active duty. Then they were paid on the same basis as National Guard members on similar duty.

The Florida statute initially designated these forces as "Florida Defense Force." However, the law was amended in May 1943 to adopt the name "Florida State Guard."

The Florida State Guard was organized into seven battalions in twenty-nine Florida communities. Total strength reached 2,097 at the end of 1944. Many of the first recruits were World War I veterans and other individuals not qualified for active federal service. A program of progressive training was established. Units were assembled for a minimum of two hours drill and instructions at local armories each week. These drills were a form of basic training to prepare members for combat duty and included riot formations. Because of extensive turnover, recruit training was a necessity at all times. However, a nucleus of well-trained non-commissioned officers kept the units in a reasonable state of readiness.

Limited budgets made it impossible to assemble the entire Florida State Guard for training but 337 officers and non-commissioned officers were trained at Camp Blanding for one-week schools August 6—13, 1944. The camp commander and staff assisted with this training on Camp Blanding facilities. The training stressed problems pertaining to internal security. The men fired rifles, machine guns and Thompson sub-machine guns and toured training facilities of the Infantry Replacement Training Center.

Major General Albert H. Blanding, for whom Camp Blanding was named, visited the post to inspect the training of the State Guard. He was then serving on active duty by appointment of Governor Spessard L. Holland as Coordinating Director of Action Divisions of the State Defense Council. This training was pronounced a success and put into active use less than a month later when 250 men from seven units were deployed to prevent a riot feared at the time of a rape trial. The trial was moved to another city, and another 300 men were called from nine units. They accomplished their mission. No riot ensued, and the accused confessed to the crime.

The Florida State Guard continued in existence as long as it was needed while the National Guard was being reconstituted in 1946. Members returned to Camp Blanding for another training session June 16-22, 1946. Four units were called to state active duty on the occasion of a hurricane disaster October 7, 1946.

When the Florida State Guard was terminated, Governor Millard Caldwell expressed appreciation to each member for their patriotic service. The Adjutant General, Brig Gen. Vivian Collins, reported that this force "reached a high state of military efficiency, and the state has at all times been assured of dependable aid to civil authorities for any emergency which might arise."

Major General Blanding (left), probably at Camp Blanding in 1940. He is still in uniform and commanding the 31st Division. Brigadiar General Vivin B. Colins, Adj. General, is on his left. The remaining officers are wearing state headquarters patches so they are General Collins' staff, not General Blanding's.

CAMP BLANDING'S GOOD CITIZENS

World War II united Americans like no other war before or since. Millions of young men willingly entered military service; women took production jobs in defense industries or joined the armed forces; families saved kitchen fat, scrap metal and old newspapers—united in the national war effort. Military and civilian citizens of Camp Blanding, already engaged full-time in the war effort, nevertheless participated actively in the same kind of patriotic endeavors as the citizens of surrounding communities.

When national War Bond drives were held, Camp Blanding was a major producer of bond sales through both payroll allotments and cash sales. In the Sixth War Loan Drive in November and December 1944, war bond sales on Camp Blanding totaled $1,091,101, including $910,140 from the IRTC, $139,000 from civilian personnel, and $41,961 from Army Service Forces military personnel.

For the Seventh War Loan Drive in June 1945, total sales more than doubled the previous drive and doubled the Camp Blanding quota. The total was $2,581,452 of which $2,147,955 came from the IRTC and $433,497 from Station Complement military and civilian personnel. The sales figures for both drives include only **increases** in bond allotments and additional cash sales. Existing bond allotments were not counted in the totals for each campaign.

In addition to buying bonds themselves, Camp Blanding personnel helped the campaign. WACs worked as pairs helping sell bonds at the post exchanges and three bands of the IRTC performed at four giant bond rallies in nearby communities.

Major efforts of the American Red Cross were directed to the armed forces, and military members responded to the Red Cross fund drives as generously as their relatively low pay permitted. The 1944 drive, for example, received contributions of $35,209 from Camp Blanding, of which $30,294 came from military personnel of the Infantry Replacement Training Center.

While civilians made major efforts to collect materials recyclable into war materiel, Camp Blanding personnel received commendations for salvage of all types of materials and sales of items which could not be re-used by the military. For the year 1944 Camp Blanding set records by collecting 1,000 tons of waste paper and selling it for $20,000, collecting and selling $82,421 worth of kitchen waste. The post collected 1,000 tons of tin cans urgently needed for war production. The total value of the extensive salvage program on the post for 1944 was $2,434,632.

Individual ingenuity resulted in savings from use of scrap materials to produce needed items for the post. Megaphones were made from sheets of galvanized iron from old footlockers. Wedges used to lock machine guns in place to protect troops from low level firing on the infiltration course were made from old axe handles. Old helmet liners and repaired clothes provided uniforms for enemy dummies on the infiltration course.

Dental clinics on the post salvaged waste gold from old fillings, collected it and sent it under guard to the United States Mint for re-use when the collection reached 900 ounces.

As with bond sales troops helped the salvage effort in nearby communities. In April 1944 one hundred troops from the Station Complement braved a rainstorm and collected 200 tons of waste paper in a citywide curbstone pick-up campaign in Jacksonville. Helped by police and Boy Scouts, the soldiers drove thirty-two trucks all day long. It was part of a national Waste Paper Victory Campaign.

Camp Blanding WACs were active in off-post public service. They gave blood regularly to the hospital, drove jeeps in Jacksonville to provide rewards to children who helped with the paper salvage campaign, and drove jeeps in a precision drill as part of a war bond drive program at Jacksonville Municipal Stadium.

Civilians grew victory gardens to help produce needed food. Camp Blanding did the same. Beginning in late 1944 and continuing in 1945, a forty-acre plot on post became the Camp Blanding "victory garden" with sweet potatoes, corn, field peas, snapbeans, eggplant and okra. The produce was used in mess halls, saving money and easing pressure on the civilian food supply.

Looking to post-war Camp Blanding as a recreation site, Master Sergeant Cecil C. Talbot of post headquarters secured 200,000 fingerling fish from Florida State Hatcheries and re-stocked six lakes on the post.

The Camp Blanding installation proved itself to be a good citizen when a hurricane threatened the post in October 1944. The Field House was thrown open to civilian and military families as a refuge from the threatened storm. Families on the perimeter of Kingsley Lake came into the post bringing children, dogs and family effects to spend the night in safety. Military personnel arranged bedding and set up a small "post exchange" to provide milk and sandwiches. When power was turned back on, they got soup and hot coffee. The Motor Pool provided bus service back to their homes for the civilians who took shelter in the Field House.

OFF-DUTY TIME

World War II Camp Blanding brought together thousands of young men and hundreds of young women far from their homes. They were united only in their common efforts on behalf of the national war effort. They made new friendships that in thousands of cases lasted the rest of their lives.

It was a controlled environment but it offered the fullest possible support for a pleasant wholesome lifestyle. Facilities on post offered entertainment, frequent social functions, sports participation, religious services, libraries and shopping. Eight theaters showed first-run movies for fifteen cents. Beer was available at post exchanges but only in 3.2 percent alcohol.

Off-post the neighboring communities of Starke and Green Cove Springs and the cities of Jacksonville, St. Augustine and Gainesville welcomed soldiers and treated them well. The Gainesville Chamber of Commerce, for example, commented in its publication in January 1944 that the soldiers "are all received cordially, treated fairly and made to feel that this town is Florida's friendly city....We like the army and the army likes us." Civilian restaurants in all these cities and towns were particularly attractive to the soldiers.

Both the Station Complement and the major troop commanders were as liberal with passes as their missions permitted. Army bus service on the post was free of charge. Bus fare to Starke was fifteen cents, to Gainesville sixty-five cents and to Jacksonville one-dollar.

In late 1944 a survey showed an average of 5,000 soldiers left the post on Saturdays for "week-end passes" to nearby cities. They spent more than $21,000 per weekend. They traveled more than a half million miles and spent $10,000 for meals alone.

USO shows on the post always drew large audiences. Performances by Jack Teagarden in 1944 and Sammy Kaye in 1945 drew audiences that filled the giant field house for dancing and national network radio broadcasts. Visits by authors such as Marjorie Kinnan Rawlings from nearby Cross Creek added cultural fare. In addition to such major occasions, dances and other social functions were held frequently at service clubs and NCO clubs throughout the post.

Officers too attended dinners given for them by the commanding general. Invitations were by memorandum specifying the date when "all officers of the Station Complement...will be present for a dinner..." On one such occasion the Headquarters officers built a huge pipe several feet long for presentation to Brig Gen. Kunzig who was well known as a MacArthur type pipe smoker. Of course, they got his permission to present it.

Practical jokes were common among the officers. A second lieutenant, summoned to the Station Complement commander's office, found the entire staff seated with one open chair. He took a seat but the colonel barked "Who told you to sit? Stand at attention." Brandishing an official-looking paper, the colonel said "I've received this document concerning you from the War Department. What have you to say for yourself?" The paper was his promotion orders.

When movie star Cary Grant visited the Camp Blanding regional station hospital in February 1945, he visited almost everyone in the hospital and signed 210 autographs. The hospital correspondent for the post newspaper wrote that Grant was a "swell guy."

Famous sports figures also visited Camp Blanding. Major League Baseball Hall of Fame stars Babe Ruth and Bobby Feller visited in 1941. Other sports visitors included heavyweight boxing champion Sgt. Joe Louis with a sparring partner for an exhibition, trick-shot golfer Joe Kirkwood and wrestler Ed "Strangler" Lewis.

One disappointment to the post public relations staff was that Bob Hope never visited Camp Blanding, the largest military post in Florida, on his visits to the state, presumably because of its remote location. One of the public relations officers volunteered to command a troop train to New York City to plead the case to Bob Hope's agency for a Blanding visit, but on that day Hiroshima was bombed.

Libraries in all Camp Blanding service clubs were well stocked with books popular among the troops. In her weekly column in the post newspaper, librarian Elinor Evans recorded the most popular books on the post in its first four years. In 1941 the most popular were *Oliver Wiswell, For Whom the Bell Tolls* and *See Here, Private Hargrove.* In 1942 the most popular were *Kings Row, The Moon Is Down* and *Blood, Sweat and Tears.* In 1943 the most requests were for *The Robe, Under Cover, So Little Time* and *One World.* In 1944 the most popular were *Good Night, Sweet Prince, The Razor's Edge, A Tree Grows in Brooklyn* and *Strange Fruit.*

The Camp Blanding Station Complement published a weekly post newspaper *The Camp Blanding Report* beginning April 5, 1944 and continuing until the war ended. Sergeant Russell R. McGuire was the editor from its inception to September 1945. Captain Leon S. Theil was post Public Relations Officer for all of the same period. The paper had regular correspondents in all the Station Complement agencies. Their writings were like "neighborhood news" columns in small town newspapers with many personal items in a highly informal style.

The newspaper, especially the unit columns, served to unite the personnel in a kind of family relationship. The troops were able to laugh at themselves through these columns. For example, the Supply Detachment correspondent wrote: "If you think M/Sgt. Moore can't double time you should have seen him step down the main drag at Penney Farms with a slightly angry cow close behind. When his wind gave out the old Signal Corps training came in handy and 'Pop' did a mighty fancy job of tree climbing."

When the Supply Detachment had a close order drill exercise, the same correspondent quoted their captain this way: "I have seen the Manual of Arms done ninty different ways but never like this. Now I have seen everything," then quoted the First Sgt. this way: "I've taught the Pygmies of Panama the Manual of the Blow Gun and it's a terrible thing to behold—boys, this reminds me of Panama."

The Headquarters Detachment correspondent wrote: "We've seen a lot of pin-up girls but the pin-up girl that occupies a choice spot over Clifford Heil's bunk takes the cheesecake. She has big brown eyes and a soulful expression...her name is Josephine and she has poise, she has breeding and she yields four gallons of milk per day....Josephine is the Heil Holstein heifer." The owner said, "Josephine symbolizes everything that I am fighting for."

The Military Police correspondent wrote about an incident when an IRTC sergeant "who never should have had that last beer" could not find his own unit. The MP drove the sergeant to his unit. On arrival they shook hands and the sergeant said "Would you believe it, I'm in the army twenty years, and this is the first time I have ever shaken an MP's hand."

The newspaper duly reported the many dances and other events scheduled on the post and almost every week announced weddings of WACs, mostly to other soldiers on post.

The story did not make the post newspaper but the public relations officer remembers what happened when orders came down that all "desk officers" would have to qualify with the rifle. One officer fired for two and half-hours without getting a qualifying score. Finally the range officer phoned the sergeant in the pits to say, "Whatever you see on the target, I want 138 on the next round."

The newspaper had its own problems when the *Gainesville Daily Sun* had to discontinue printing the newspaper because of its "shortage of manpower." The *St. Augustine Record* came to the rescue by agreeing to print the paper at $107 for 5,000 copies of the four-page paper, a price that seems a pittance today.

The many friendships formed at Camp Blanding resulted in social visits for many years. One such visit went awry in 1944 when Lt. R.L. Strickler, former commander of Headquarters Detachment No. 1, came back to Camp Blanding to visit his old outfit. At the same time First Sgt. Palmer Sills and Tech Sgt. Charles Danley left Camp Blanding the day before for the express purpose of dropping in on Lt. Strickler at Fort Bragg which was near their homes. They returned to Blanding the day after the lieutenant departed for his post at Fort Bragg.

More than fifty years later veterans of World War II are returning to Camp Blanding to visit the Museum and Memorial Park, always emotionally touched by the displays and the audio tapes made for the museum by veterans who served at

Camp Blanding. Their reactions were depicted by veteran Carson Kirk in a newspaper column in 1992 in the *Powell Valley News*, reproduced at page 201.

The Reynolds chapel as it exists today at Camp Blanding.

WINDING DOWN

In addition to its training missions throughout the war, Camp Blanding played important roles in Army Personnel Management. The Reception Center was activated November 15, 1940. When the war ended, it had accepted more than 90,000 Floridians into the army. The station processed the individual's paperwork, gave him an army classification and issued clothing and some items of equipment.

With war's end in Europe, the return of troops to the states for discharge or re-deployment to the Pacific Theater became a priority mission of major proportions. The same reasons of climate and terrain that made the Southeastern area of the country most suitable for assembling and training the early divisions made the area, including Camp Blanding, ideal for the new missions. This entailed major supply operations including procurement and issue of thousands of uniforms and items of equipment, feeding a heavy flow of personnel and providing an appropriate environment for returning combat veterans.

The army established a War Department Personnel Center at Camp Blanding with multiple functions in the process.

It required conversion of several buildings in the Infantry Replacement Training Center and in the old Reception Center. The Reception Center had closed February 19, 1944, but an Induction Station had continued to operate at a lower tempo. The contract for work on the buildings went to J. L. Ewell of Lakeland with the work supervised by the Army District Engineer's Office in Savannah.

The first element of the new Personnel Center to go into operation was the AirLift Disposition Center. Its mission was to process selected men returning from the European Theater of Operations by Air Transport Command planes to Miami. Upon their arrival in Miami, these men immediately boarded shuttle trains to Camp Blanding thus avoiding delays which would have ensued from unavoidable crowding due to lack of staging area space in the Miami air terminal area.

These men began arriving at Camp Blanding June 5, 1945. They departed within thirty-six hours to the reception station nearest their homes to begin a thirty-day furlough. These men had selected their desired reception station before leaving their overseas station. At Camp Blanding they received an initial orientation talk, physical examination and cigarette ration card. Those who needed money were given a partial payment of ten dollars at Camp Blanding. That was a useful amount in 1945. This AirLift Disposition Center was referred to as the "Green Project." Its main element was speed.

The "Green Project" airlifts ended September 10, 1945. By this time Camp Blanding had received and processed 55,534 enlisted men and 3,240 officers arriving by airlift via Miami. The process continued at Camp Blanding, however, under the name "Rainbow Project" to process thousands of returning Air Transport Command personnel who had operated the overseas "Green Project" as well as the "White Project" for personnel flown home by their units and "Red Project" air service for liberated American prisoners of war.

When Brigadier General Robert S. Israel, Jr., became the Camp Blanding commander in July 1945, he also assumed command of the Personnel Center in accord with War Department policy that this important activity be commanded by a general officer.

The Personnel Center consisted of four major divisions: the Disposition Center, discussed above; a reception station to classify all returning Floridians and some other individuals for discharge or furlough before assignment to new duty; the Separation Center to process Floridians being discharged, and an induction station to examine and induct Floridians for Army service. The following chart shows the organization structure:

{**PERSONNEL CENTER**}

Air Lift Disposition Center	Reception Station	Separation Center	Induction Station
Flown from Europe, re-routed to reception stations near homes	Classified for discharge or furlough and new duty	Processed for discharge	Civilians going into service

Every effort was made at Camp Blanding to provide an appropriate environment for returning combat veterans. Immediately upon activation of the Personnel Center, a new post exchange was established in two buildings in the Center to provide food and drink along with many items returning soldiers would want especially gifts to take home. By the end of October 1945, that post exchange was doing more than double the volume of business of any other exchange on the post, selling 1,200 hamburgers and hot dogs a day, 125 cases of soft drinks and 200 to 300 cartons of cigarettes. It included a three-chair barbershop.

The mess hall in the Personnel Center had fifty cooks to feed 1,500 to 2,000 persons at each meal. The effort there was to provide "food like Mother makes—when she can get the points" (referring to the rationing system for civilians throughout the war).

Recreation facilities were provided also for use of returning veterans during their short stays at Camp Blanding. A beach area was cleared, truckloads of sand were hauled in, and a pier and diving board were set up. Athletic equipment, magazines and games were available to all. The post office established a branch in the Personnel Center to provide full postal services and to explain postage rates and regulations.

In its first three weeks of operation, the Camp Blanding Reception Station processed 2,224 men, of whom 550 were routed to the Separation Center for discharge. This process continued as long as troops were being processed for re-deployment to the Pacific for an estimated total of about 5,000.

By October 1, 1945, with the war in the Pacific over, the Camp Blanding Separation Center had discharged 10,000 returning Florida veterans (and a few from other states). The Separation Center had grown to an organization of about 800 personnel capable of processing 300 to 400 men and women per day for discharge.

Because so many personnel of the IRTC were eligible for discharge, the Personnel Center established a branch Separation Center in the IRTC area with capability of discharging 200 men per day.

Soldiers being processed for discharge received a pamphlet welcoming them to Camp Blanding and providing information about facilities at the post, the discharge process and veterans' rights. The army was interested in maintaining a reserve force after World War II. The Camp Blanding Personnel Center set up a special section to provide information about the Enlisted Reserve Corps. Returning officers were invited to join the Organized Reserve Corps. A War Department "Memorandum for All Officers" dated twenty-four August 1945 and signed by President Harry S. Truman. To make his point forcefully, his signature block on this memorandum was "Colonel, Field Artillery Reserve."

As the activities at Camp Blanding wound down, former Sergeant Julian K. Wood recalls a night when substantially all the remaining troops departed leaving behind all their property except weapons and vehicles. He says they left their clothing and equipment and their supply rooms full. Then a detail of 200 men, some of whom were prisoners of war, worked for two weeks with a fleet of trucks hauling many tons of supplies including food, bedding and kitchenware, to the range area and burying it. He considered this an extremely wasteful policy to prevent flooding the civilian market. He got permission to retrieve a few items for his personal use. He says today he still has two footlockers and still uses stainless steel tableware and an ax that he saved from burial.

Many who served at Camp Blanding were so attracted to the area that they remained after the war. Sergeant Ben Zellner came to Camp Blanding in 1941 from the motor maintenance school at Fort Benning, remained to operate the same training school while his wife worked in the purchasing agent's office. After the war he was in the automobile business in Green Cove Springs and became mayor of that city. After his death his wife received her Ph.D. in education and still lives at Penney Farms. She recalls that the big house on S.R. 16 in Penney Farms was once a luxury hotel and became an apartment house where some officers and their wives lived.

George (Tiny) Lovell came to Camp Blanding in 1942, married a local girl and never left the area despite some not-so-happy experiences. It was very cold the night he arrived, but no blankets were available. Instead he got two mattresses and slept between them the first night. He was assigned to the 30th Division but the day the unit was scheduled to depart he was ordered to take an injured soldier to the hospital. On the way the ambulance was in a wreck injuring Lovell's foot. He remained in the Station Complement.

In World War II Camp Blanding touched the lives of hundreds of thousands of persons—almost all favorably. Precise totals cannot be calculated but a reasonable summary would look like this:

PERSONNEL AT CAMP BLANDING IN WORLD WAR II

Nine Army divisions
(including many replacements
for departing cadre, officer candidates and Army Air Force transfers) 175,000

508th Parachute Infantry
(total interviewed) 4,500

Other non-divisional units 32,000

Station Complement 10,000

IRTC Trainees 200,000

IRTC Cadre 6,000

Hospital Patients
(from other posts or
returnees from overseas) 8,000

POW Camp Cadre 500

Prisoners of War 4,686

Inductions (including those rejected) 130,000

Florida State Guard	**500**
War Dept Personnel Center (1945)**Staff**	**5,000**
"Green Project" Returnees	**58,774**
"White" and "Red" Projects Returnees	**10,000**
Reception Station Returnees	**5,000**
Discharges	**12,000**
Separation Center Staff	**800**
Red Cross, Post Office and IRS Personnel	**1,000**
Construction Workers Building the Camp	**21,000**
Post Civilian Employees (including attrition)	**10,000**
Visitors to Guest Houses	**50,000**
Visiting USO Shows Personnel	**500**
TOTAL	**745,260**

Almost none of the above figures can be calculated precisely. They represent the authors' best estimates. Added to the above total should be the thousands of family members of Camp Blanding personnel who lived in the surrounding communities. Uncounted numbers of other persons visited Camp Blanding including those delivering supplies, casual local visitors such as thousands attending public ceremonies, media representatives and visiting military personnel on official business. Even with some duplication in the categories in the table above, we can safely conclude that Camp Blanding touched the lives of at least a million persons during World War II.

WAR DEPARTMENT,
WASHINGTON 25, D. C., 24 August 1945.

MEMORANDUM FOR ALL OFFICERS

ORGANIZED RESERVE CORPS

THE WHITE HOUSE,
Washington, August 20, 1945.

To All Servicemen:

Our country, which you have served so well, needs your continued patriotic support in the Organized Reserve Corps.

When you leave the service, I am personally interested that, as an enlisted man, you enlist in the Reserves, or that, as an officer, you accept a new commission in the Officers' Reserve Corps. In so doing you will contribute to the future security of our country immeasurably.

Colonel, Field Artillery Reserve.

MEMORIES

Contacts with World War II veterans for this book brought a flood of memories of Camp Blanding, almost all positive in nature.

"Tough" was the most commonly used word to describe basic training at Camp Blanding, whether in the combat divisions or the Infantry Replacement Training Center. Almost to a man they said that experience brought them to the best physical condition of their lives and taught them teamwork.

James V. Maguire of Wakefield, MA, remembers his company commander, Lt. Warren Fox, Company E, 119th Infantry, as an outstanding leader who "trained us at Camp Blanding and eventually led us into combat in June 1944.... We became close and we were a good team." Lieutenant Fox was killed in action during the 30th Division's heavy combat in Europe. Maguire still keeps in touch with some of his World War II colleagues.

Robert B. Bradley of Gettysburg, PA, was a medical enlisted man in the 30th Division at Camp Blanding. He says, "the army certainly prolonged my life." He praised his combat training at Camp Blanding. Bradley has written and published a series of poems about his wartime army experience. His most recent publication is "The Aidman-Infantry Team" with sections dealing with the 30th Division's experiences in Europe. Copies are in the Camp Blanding Museum archives.

No set of memories of wartime experiences would be complete without recollections of KP. Kitchen Police was a duty every soldier had to perform occasionally. It involved helping prepare food, serve meals and clean up the mess hall. Kris Dalane of Charlotte, N.C., says, "one of the toughest chores we had was K.P. "The C.Q. (an NCO on duty overnight in Charge of Quarters) would wake you up at 4:30AM, and you worked until about 10:00PM at night. You walked back to your bunk and fell asleep in a second." He also adds that "the food we got at Camp Blanding was the very best we ever got in the army, especially hot cakes for breakfast and chicken dinner at noon on Sunday."

Upon arrival at Camp Blanding some newly inducted men found the post foreboding and dismal at first sight. Henry M. (Hank) Stairs of Ligonier, PA, remembers arriving in the dark by train from New Cumberland, PA. He says he sank ankle-deep in sand and said to his new G.I. friend "Why would they haul all this sand and dump it here on the railroad siding?"

Others saw it differently. Robert L. Wilson of Miami, FL, remembers it this way: "I was pulling KP in the kitchen car of a troop train from Camp Breckenridge, KY. In the first light of dawn I stood in the open door of the kitchen car and saw the scrub palmettos, the pines, and the sand that is characteristic of North Florida. There was a smell of pine in the air and everything looked clean and fresh. It made such an impression on me that I resolved to some day live in Florida...but it took me twenty-three more years to achieve that goal."

His memories of the rest of his time at Camp Blanding confirmed that first impression. Wilson says "Camp Blanding was a joy....The hutments were a pleasant contrast from the conventional two story barracks. Cleaning our quarters was a breeze...just sweep out the sand in the morning and we were ready for inspection." After the war he became an FBI agent and served in many areas of the country before returning to Florida.

Soldiers at Camp Blanding had a wide variety of experiences.

Salvatore Bazzano of Yonkers, NY, shared a one-room garage unit with two friends, Robert Sullivan and Lou Santucci. He had the job of repairing and refinishing furniture. He remembers his work on furniture for the Officers Club, the 120th Infantry Recreation Room and a bedroom for Col. Hammond D. Birk. He says now "I made many new friends and I have good memories of the camp. I hope some day I will revisit Camp Blanding."

Tom L. Raney of Fairfax Station, VA, vividly recalls an incident when he found that someone had broken his Big Ben alarm clock. His tentmates identified the culprit and Raney invited him out to "Fist City." The fight lasted a half-hour, both were exhausted, and they pronounced it a draw. Raney had several marks on his face. The First Sergeant, a no-nonsense NCO of the old school, told him he had done the right thing. Raney tells the rest of the story this way: "A few days later I was notified that I was to appear before the camp's OCS (Officer Candidate School) Board. One of the troop's 'guardhouse lawyers' advised me to tell the Board that our regiment had been recently reorganized as a mechanized outfit and I'd had a spill with a motorcycle. The Board consisted of five older field grade officers. The only question I remember was 'What happened to your face, Sergeant?' I told them the truth, exactly as related above. I figured it was nothing to be ashamed of. At any rate, the Board approved my application and in April, I departed for Fort Riley, Kansas." Tom Raney was commissioned and served to retire from the army as a Colonel.

Sidney Eichen of Hollywood, FL, was a lieutenant in the 120th Infantry at Camp Blanding. He has fond memories of his experiences as a basketball player and coach, still considers himself a basketball "junkie." When the 1943 basketball season began, Colonel Birk (who had a reputation as a sports fanatic) asked Eichen if he would like to "try to coach the regimental team in the division tournament."

Eichen gladly accepted and proved he could do much more than "try to coach." The team swept the opposition and won the camp tournament. The team even let Lt. Eichen play. The colonel approved, even diagrammed plays occasionally on the tablecloth in the officers mess. Including free lance games, the 120th team won twenty-two and lost three. The losses were to the University of Florida at Gainesville, the Jacksonville Naval Air Station and a split of two games with the 508th Parachute Infantry.

William A. Pillsbury of Lutherville, MD, was part of the 63rd Division cadre. While waiting for their filler troops (who never reached Camp Blanding), the cadre spent hours practicing rifle marksmanship with dummy ammunition in the areas between the hutments. He remembers "an occasion when a bullet went through the screen of a hutment right next to a soldier who was shaving. No one ever discovered how a live round ever got into the dummy ammo."

As a disciplined soldier Pillsbury had an unnerving experience when he and Sgt. Owen Duff were chosen to pose for a photograph in the Division newspaper *Blood and Fire.* The paper wanted a photo of two soldiers saluting General Hibbs.

Here's what happened: "We walked toward the General as he walked toward us and at the proper moment, we saluted. To my horror, I discovered that I was too close to Duff and my salute therefore was given with my elbow against my body. The picture, thank God, only showed Duff's and my backs because it clearly revealed the awful salute. I held my breath for a month but nothing ever came of it."

Soon after the United States entered the war, the city of Jacksonville honored ten men of the 43rd Division and ten of the 31st Division as "outstanding soldiers." Mayor John T. Alsop presented city scrolls to each soldier at a luncheon. One of the 43rd Division men was Sgt. Earl A. Taylor of Dennisport, MA, then serving in Battery D, 192nd Field Artillery. Two gun crews on maneuvers cited him for outstanding work.

Sgt. Taylor remembers another incident when a composite battery of the 192nd Field Artillery participated in a pickle festival at Wachula, FL. He was selected as one to be guest of a local family. He says "The people I went home with were true Southerners, making me feel very welcome with their gracious welcome in their home—except Grandfather, sitting in his rocker in the living room, asked where I was from. When I replied Connecticut, all he said was "Damn Yankee" and that was his last word to me. The family was embarrassed even though "I kinda thought it was funny."

Former First Sergeant William G. Smith Sr. of Madison, OH, was selected to attend lifeguard school while the 63rd Division cadre awaited its troops. He was the smallest man in the class, weighing about 130, fifty pounds less than his class partner. At the end of the training each man had to go down fifteen feet, pick up his partner, carry him to shore and apply first aid. Says First Sgt. "Smitty"—"I really struggled to carry him, but did. That evening when we were all dressed in our uniforms for graduation, our instructor was really surprised we were all senior NCOs and one lieutenant who was my partner."

The infiltration course at Camp Blanding brought vivid recollections for many veterans. Crawling under live machine gun fire is an experience not easily forgotten. Frank R. Vogel of Fort Myers, FL, got in trouble after crawling through the course. He placed his M-1 rifle against a pine tree, removed his jacket to shake out the mud, and then forgot on which tree he had placed his rifle. He rightly remembers that "to lose one's rifle is a truly traumatic experience." His sergeant found the rifle. Vogel describes the result: "The dressing down I received was a sight to behold. My punishment—to sleep with six M-1 rifles for the period of one week. The CQ checked three or four times each night to make sure they hadn't 'fallen' out of my bunk."

Frank Vogel also remembers that a unit of Nisei (Japanese-Americans) were adjacent to his battalion during basic training in the IRTC. His comments: "We were told—and for the life of me I didn't understand why—not to fraternize with the so-called 'Japs.' I figured most of them were probably more American than I. I was a second generation American of German descent."

The Japanese-American trainees drew considerable gossip on the post. They were said to be the hardest-working training unit. Later overseas they became part of the Japanese-American units that gained distinction in combat in Italy.

Hank Stairs, the soldier who wondered about the sand beside the rail siding, was in the 66th Division. The 30th Division was there at the same time. Later, in the hedgerows of Normandy, he and several other ex-66th Division members joined the 30th Division as replacements just in time for a baptism of fire at Mortain. He wonders what other 66th Division buddies also saw combat with the 30th Division. He knows two who were killed in action.

Although the preponderance of memories of Camp Blanding are favorable, one unfortunate incident had serious adverse consequences. James F. Hammond of Corry, PA, was a member of the 30th Quartermaster Company of the 30th Division. Members of that unit were briefly exposed to mustard gas during a training exercise in early 1943. After the war Hammond suffered chronic bronchitis, repeated bouts of pneumonia and other respiratory problems. He persistently presented his case to the Veterans Administration as a service-connected disability. After fifty years, he succeeded in getting formal acknowledgement by VA in 1994 and a small disability compensation.

Walter M. Morawski of Pittsfield, MA, reports that he also was exposed to mustard gas with post-war consequences affecting both eyes. Contact lenses and surgery eventually corrected his problems. Despite this experience, Hammond still has "lots of good memories of Camp Blanding—good friends, very good facilities and training." He says he enjoyed visits to Starke, Daytona Beach, Jacksonville, Silver Springs, St. Augustine, West Palm Beach and Cocoa Beach. Morawski also has good memories of Camp Blanding, saying "basic training was rough but I loved it." He received a medical discharge later in 1943.

Wives of soldiers who could find and afford local housing developed a camaraderie that in many cases survives today. Helen S. Black of Kansas City, MO, recalls the good times she and her late husband Robert Black had while at Camp Blanding. They found housing in a four-plex owned by a Bible group. Their upper apartment neighbors were George and Elise Wilson. Both couples consisted of one southerner and one northerner. This made it a happy opportunity to eat together frequently to provide the kind of food everybody liked. The ladies had a habit of sunning topless until a plane circled their area frequently and Captain Black told his wife the plane was "surveying the territory."

Comments in these letters reflect the same attitude displayed by scores of World War II veterans now participating as volunteers in the Camp Blanding Museum project. All are eager to preserve for posterity the historical heritage depicted by the artifacts now on display at Camp Blanding.

END OF THE WAR

All over the world, 1945 was an eventful year. World War II ended, and nations began converting from a wartime economy to normal civilian pursuits. In the United States millions were released from the Armed Forces to pursue their lives in a supply-and-demand economy. Even before Japan surrendered, the United States began planning its post-war military establishment. These plans would present new problems for Camp Blanding and the Florida National Guard.

The War Department faced the problem of deciding which bases should be retained for the post-war army. This task was assigned to the Office of the Chief of Engineers who conducted a series of *Post-War Utilization Studies* including an analysis of Camp Blanding, Florida in September 1945.

The analysis was based on regional factors, physical development of the post and training facilities. In all of these sections Camp Blanding received high marks on many important factors.

REGIONAL FACTORS noted were recreational and cultural facilities, moderate climate with negligible training time lost to adverse weather, health and comfort of troops and no flooding of critical post areas at any time. No adverse factors were noted.

POST DEVELOPMENT was described in terms of existing construction and future needs. It noted that 54,920 troops were housed in hutments and 1,207 in Theater of Operations type construction. Housing conditions were found unsatisfactory in respect to fire prevention. Water supply system, electric power and sewage disposal facilities were found satisfactory. Rail service was found to be not entirely satisfactory, highway system good and adequate for post-war use. Total cost of Camp Blanding to the government since July 1, 1940 was shown to be approximately $42,526,000.

TRAINING FACILITIES were described favorably in every respect including accessibility to small arms ranges, topography for artillery firing, maneuver areas for training, review and drill grounds, accessibility to nearby Keystone Army Air Base and facilities for engineering training.

After identifying these criteria for retention of Camp Blanding, the Engineers' report concluded with the following comment:

> "From an engineering standpoint Camp Blanding is not considered satisfactory for post-war retention for the following reasons: (1) The housing is predominantly hutment-type construction and considerable cost would be entailed in providing a new permanent housing development. (2) Rail facilities are too light for a permanent installation and would have to be replaced by heavier rail. In addition to required improvements to railroad and sewage disposal facilities and based on the assumptions given in the attached appendix, the cost of provid-

ing permanent bachelor officers'quarters and new barracks for 7,883 enlisted personnel would be in the neighborhood of $18,000,000. The cost of remodeling the relatively few mobilization type barracks for the postwar use of 522 enlisted personnel is included in the above amount."

From the perspective of fifty years later and the usefulness of Camp Blanding continuing to the present, the estimated cost would seem to have been a bargain. However, Camp Blanding survived through the initiative of Florida leaders and subsequent arrangements with the War Department.

This War Department decision launched what we term the "Tear Down Period" for Camp Blanding.

A squad of trainees posed in their dress uniforms in 1944. This was the 1st squad, 2nd platoon, Company D, 203rd Infantry Training Battallion of the Infantry Replacement Training Center.

THE YEARS AFTER WORLD WAR II

With the decision that Camp Blanding would not be a federal installation in the post-war army, the War Department began the task of restoring leased lands to their previous conditions for return to their former owners. This was a major task because of the many parcels of land leased from Clay County citizens.

The 30,000 acres originally acquired by the state of Florida were returned to state control. The Armory Board recognized the need for a National Guard training site would be just as great as it was when the land was acquired to replace Camp Foster, the previous training site. The state requested and received title to improvements on this land in lieu of restoring it to its previous condition. These included the road system, the sewer system, part of the water works, the cold storage warehouses, maintenance shops, the field house and several residences.

These acquisitions were integrated into the post-war Camp Blanding. The field house became an auditorium and later a warehouse for post, camp and station property. This building was destroyed by fire in 1977.

Among the residences were eight general officers quarters overlooking the parade field. Five two-story homes were built to the same specifications except two, which had larger interior floor plans. Those two are now on Avenue A. Three of the small houses were relocated to the lake-front on each side of the small creek that runs underneath Avenue A. Those three houses were used by employees of the maintenance shops from 1948 to 1960. Three other homes are now located on Avenue B. One is at the old Main Gate where Avenue B terminates at S.R. 16. Another is at the south end of the post exchange building. The third is on Avenue B next to the post chapel. Col. Harry Hatcher lived in this home from 1949 to 1959.

THE TEAR DOWN PERIOD

Then began the task of dismantling, selling or salvaging the rest of the buildings on the post. The Army Camp Wrecking Corporation took more than three years to complete this mission. Considerable ingenuity was displayed in converting many old structures to new uses at new locations to the benefit of the army and the buyers.

The best example of this is related by Col. Harry M. Hatcher Jr., (Ret.) of Starke, (who later became Camp Blanding post commander). The buildings were offered for sale in 1947 to the highest bidders, most of whom planned to tear the buildings down to salvage the materials. Successful bidders were required to dispose of the buildings they acquired within a short time—about ninety days. Hatcher and his father were interested in the main administration building of the station hospital and five adjacent nurses quarters buildings. The administration building was a U-shaped structure with the closed end of the U facing Kingsley Lake. Centered on the closed end of the building was the fountain, which now marks the entrance to post headquarters.

Probably because the hospital was so large, few bids were offered. The Hatcher bid of $2,400 for the administration building and five nurses quarters was accepted. They hired a mover named Hygema in Green Cove Springs at a cost greater than the price of the buildings. He transported the hospital in sections by truck to Middleburg, about nine miles from Camp Blanding, then loaded them on barges on Black Creek to the St. Johns River, then to Jacksonville Beach where the Hatchers converted it into a 40-unit motel. The nurses quarters were converted to multi-family residences at Jacksonville Beach. Even at a bid of $2,400, the sale benefitted the army because it eliminated the cost of tearing down the buildings.

At this time the federal government retained title to the 40,000 acres it had purchased, and the state retained title to its 30,000 acres. This situation would not change until 1954 when, after long effort by the governor, the Florida Congressional delegation and The Adjutant General, the Congress enacted legislation transferring to the state of Florida title to the 40,000 acres of federal land under conditions described below.

The years 1945 and 1946 saw the beginning of the reorganization of the Florida National Guard. The War Department authorized a strength of 691 officers and 8,933 enlisted for Florida elements of the 51st and 48th Infantry Divisions and some non-divisional units. This was 2½ times the size of the pre-war Florida National Guard. The Adjutant General warned this would require greatly increased state budgets to qualify for the federal support.

Meanwhile, the Florida State Guard could only be gradually disbanded because some troops would still be needed while the National Guard recruited its new members. The Florida State Guard trained at Camp Blanding June 16—22, 1946.

The Adjutant General's Report for 1945 and 1946 showed the value of land and buildings at Camp Blanding was $750,000. This figure, a pittance compared with the present value of the post, shows what has happened at Camp Blanding since World War II although its prospects were not bright at that time.

Although the state made some use of Camp Blanding in these years, it was not used in a major way for its original mission of training Florida National Guard troops until the state received title to the 40,000 acres of federal land. We term this interim the Dormant Period.

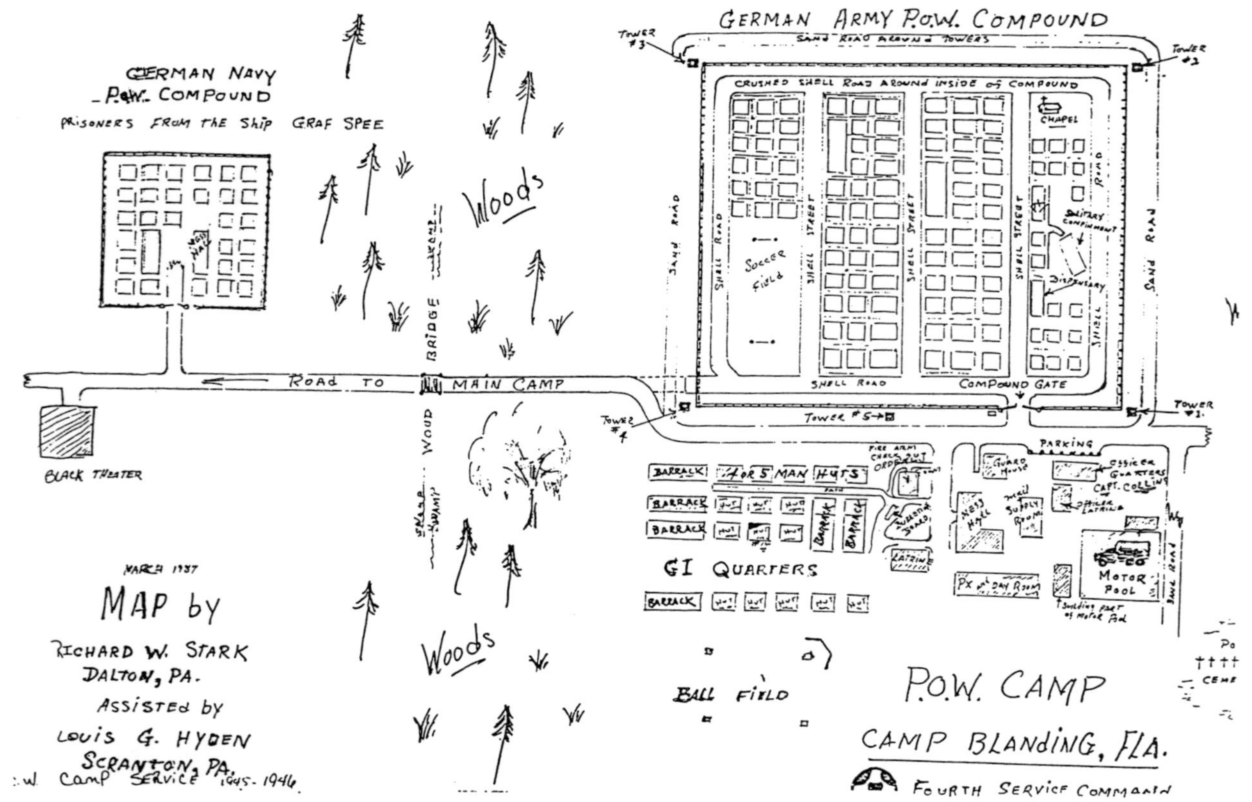

GERMAN ARMY P.O.W. COMPOUND
SAND ROAD AROUND TOWERS
TOWER #3
TOWER #2
CRUSHED SHELL ROAD AROUND INSIDE OF COMPOUND
CHAPEL
SOLITARY CONFINEMENT
DISPENSARY
SAND ROAD
SHELL ROAD
SHELL STREET
SHELL STREET
SHELL STREET
SHELL ROAD
SAND ROAD
SOCCER FIELD
SHELL ROAD
COMPOUND GATE
TOWER #5 →
TOWER #4
TOWER #1
GERMAN NAVY
P.O.W. COMPOUND
PRISONERS FROM THE SHIP GRAF SPEE
MESS HALL
Woods
BRIDGE
ROAD TO MAIN CAMP
WOOD
SPRING SWAMP
BLACK THEATER
Woods
MARCH 1937
MAP by
RICHARD W. STARK
DALTON, PA.
ASSISTED by
LOUIS G. HYDEN
SCRANTON, PA.
.W. CAMP SERVICE 1945-1946.
PARKING
FIRE ARMS CHECK OUT ORDERLY
BARRACK
4 OR 5 MAN HUTS
PATH
BARRACK
BARRACK
BARRACK
BARRACK
LATRINE
GUARD HOUSE
MESS HALL
MAIL SUPPLY ROOM
OFFICER QUARTERS
CAPT. COLLINS
OFFICER LATRINE
MOTOR POOL
building part of Motor Pool
GI QUARTERS
BARRACK
PX & DAY ROOM
BALL FIELD
Po
CEME
P.O.W. CAMP
CAMP BLANDING, FLA.
FOURTH SERVICE COMMAND

THE DORMANT PERIOD

During the years immediately after World War II, Camp Blanding's mission in support of the Florida National Guard was largely logistical. Some units used the ranges for marksmanship training and occasional command post exercises on weekends. Unit field training was conducted at Fort Jackson, SC; Fort McClellan, AL, and Fort Stewart, GA.

Camp Blanding provided major logistical support. The Concentration Site, organized early in 1949 with Captain Harry Hatcher as its supervisor, received track and wheel vehicles from army depots and other federal sources. After processing, they were issued to Florida National Guard units. The State Maintenance Shops were responsible for all ordnance equipment maintenance. All federal military equipment and supplies also were warehoused and processed at Camp Blanding.

It is appropriate to note here that Brig Gen. Vivian Collins, who served as Adjutant General of Florida throughout the war years, retired April 15, 1947, and was succeeded by Brig. Gen. Mark W. Lance.

In his report for the years 1947 and 1948, General Lance recorded that "through a cooperative working agreement with the state prison farm, approved by the Board of Commissioners of State Institutions, that portion of the (Camp Blanding) reservation not required for military operational uses has been opened as a range for raising beef cattle...under the management of the state prison farm." He said this arrangement "contributed to economies in procurement of meat for state needs."

In his report for 1949 and 1950, General Lance quoted a letter from the Superintendent of the Florida State Prison describing increased beef production and significant cost savings resulting from this arrangement.

In a similar arrangement in those years the Florida Development Commission used warehouses at Camp Blanding for storage and distribution of surplus properties to educational institutions in the state of Florida. The Commission's supervisor at Camp Blanding was Frank Beard who frequently assisted the Maintenance Shops in locating rare but urgently needed spare parts for World War II equipment. By 1949 some Regular Army, Marine Corps and Navy units were using rifle ranges at Camp Blanding, and the Navy was using one of the lakes as a bombing range.

A more significant development came in 1947 when E.I. DuPont de Nemours and Co., Inc. started negotiations for a lease to mine ilmenite, a strategic mineral, on part of the Camp Blanding property. After approval by the Trustees of the Internal Improvement Fund and the Cabinet, a lease was granted for mining operations on six sections of land. DuPont erected a plant and invested $1,000,000 in this project which would provide royalties to the Armory Board on mined minerals. This operation would be further expanded in subsequent contracts. By 1950 the value of buildings at Camp Blanding was estimated at $1,025,890.

With deterioration of the situation on the Korean peninsula, the federal government negotiated a new lease on portions of the state owned lands, then let contracts for construction that would be needed if the federal government needed Camp Blanding for an active installation. This construction included:

1. Construction of a Signal Radio and Repair Shop as part of the Combined Support Maintenance Shops.

2. Reconstruction of a railroad from Starke to the old warehouse area.

3. Rehabilitation and extension of sewage lines, sewage pumping stations and sewage disposal plant.

4. Drilling of two new wells, rehabilitation of existing wells and pump houses, rehabilitation of existing water mains, laying of new water mains and installation of new water hydrants, rehabilitation of existing elevated water tanks and construction of two new water tanks.

The land, facilities and new construction were then returned to the state on a "Right of Entry" for use by the National Guard pending possible future use by federal forces, but Camp Blanding was never needed by the federal government for the Korean War. Logistical operations on the post were not affected by this lease arrangement.

Other activities continued on the post including the prison system use of the area to raise cattle and the Florida Development Commission warehousing operations. Also a forest management program was instituted with the prison system and the Florida Board of Forestry cooperating.

Military training on the post was still confined to use of the ranges for marksmanship, command post and map exercises. Although this training was important to the Florida National Guard, it would be 1965 before Camp Blanding was

used regularly for Annual Training. Units continued to conduct their field training at Fort McClellan and Fort Stewart.
Regular forces continued to use the ranges, and the navy
continued its bombing practice at Stevens Lake.

Camp Blanding was then identified in the Adjutant
General's Report for 1951 and 1952 as a station of the Florida
National Guard. Lt. Col. James A. Griffin, State Maintenance
Officer, was post commander. Company B (Rear), 748th
Ordnance Battalion, was stationed at Camp Blanding. Cap-
tain Harry M. Hatcher, Jr., who later became the first full-
time post commander since World War II, was also stationed
at Camp Blanding as Ordnance Shop Officer.

The next biennium (1953—1954) would see major developments that eventually would lead to the rebirth and increased use of Camp Blanding.

Although the federal government had granted a "Right-
of-Entry" to federal lands on Camp Blanding for National
Guard training, the State Armory Board did not have control
of that part of the post, nor authority to exploit resources,
practice forest management and provide necessary security.
Negotiations began in 1951 to gain title to the federal lands.
With assistance of Senator Spessard L. Holland and Repre-
sentative Charles E. Bennett (in whose Congressional District
Camp Blanding was located), a bill was introduced in Congress to transfer title to the state of Florida. Because of some
misunderstandings, the bill was not passed in the 82nd Congress which adjourned in 1952.

The Adjutant General immediately proceeded to conferences with Department of the Army. As a result a new bill was
introduced in the 83rd Congress and was enacted as Public
Law 83-493, approved July 14, 1954. It was entitled "An Act
to provide for the conveyance of the federally owned lands
which are situated within Camp Blanding Military Reserva-

tion, Florida, to the Armory Board, state of Florida, in order to consolidate ownership and perpetuate the availability of Camp Blanding for military training and use."

P.L. 493 provided that the lands would be conveyed to the Armory Board after execution of an agreement between the Armory Board and the federal government covering use of revenue from exploitation of timber and minerals. It also provided for reversion to federal ownership for the duration of any future national emergency. The entire reservation was to be kept intact in order that it be available for military uses only.

The agreement required by the law was consummated January 24, 1955, and a deed transferring title to the Armory Board was executed the same day. The Armory Board was required to maintain all of Camp Blanding as a military reservation, prepare and implement a forest management plan and continue to make improvements to the property. The agreement also provided that any residue in revenue after expenditures on improvement must be divided equally between the federal government and the state of Florida at the end of each fiscal year. Timber sales began immediately, and many miles of fence and roadways were constructed.

This legislation and the ensuing agreement paved the way for future growth of Camp Blanding.

Post headquarters at Camp Blanding today on the site of the old Station Hospital of World War II days.

REBIRTH OF CAMP BLANDING

In November 1955 the48th Infantry Division was re-designated as 48th Armored Division. As part of this reorganization, the unit stationed at Camp Blanding became Company B, 748th Armored Ordnance Battalion. Lt. Col. James A. Griffin continued as post commander.

A tank range was constructed at Camp Blanding for sub-caliber firing by the newly designated 48th Armored Division. It came into use beginning May 1, 1956, for weekend firing. Other types of training continued including rifle range firing, staff conferences, map problems and unit exercises.

About this time the agreement under which the state prison farm had raised cattle at Camp Blanding was terminated. The Armory Board entered into an agreement with the Florida Game and Fresh Water Fish Commission under which portions of Camp Blanding were opened to public hunting. For the first time in many years hunting was allowed in November 1956. This practice continues in season to this date.

To carry out provisions of Public Law 493 and the Agreement with the federal government, a Camp Blanding Management Fund was established to receive the income from mining royalties and sale of timber and pulpwood. Receipts into this Fund were recorded as follows:

Fiscal year ending

30 June 1955	$ 22,520.00
30 June 1956	112,965.72
30 June 1957	118,133.00
30 June 1958	319,034.00

Detailed figures were not included in annual reports of the following years, but the Fund continued to produce significant revenue to the extent that it eventually provided all the state funding of Camp Blanding.

In 1957 another unit was added to the Camp Blanding station list: the 379th Signal Detachment (Radar Maintenance), an element of the 227th Antiaircraft Artillery Group. The detachment was commanded by CWO Lonnie L. Fullwood. Co. B, 748th Ordnance Company was then commanded by First Lt. Rodney P. Hall.

Use of Camp Blanding for military training gradually increased into the decade of the 1960s. In the years 1959 and 1960, the Florida National Guard used the ranges for ninety days with an estimated 16,500 man-days of firing. Approximately seventy-five unit weekends of field problems and command post exercises were held. In addition, the Navy, Marine Corps, Air Force and other reserve components used the ranges 265 days for an estimated 12,800 man-days of firing.

The forest management program at Camp Blanding was expanding under supervision of a full-time forester with a continuous program of timber sales and replanting for the production of new trees in a random pattern to preserve the forest usable for military training.

E.I. DuPont de Nemours and Company had been mining on Camp Blanding since an agreement was executed with the Armory Board in December 1947. On state lands DuPont had a mill and concentrating plant known as Trail Ridge Mine. In March 1955 the Armory Board entered into a supplemental agreement with DuPont for mining on the former federal lands. DuPont leased land adjoining Camp Blanding on the north and had a mine in operation on this property known as the Highland Mine. Under the new agreement DuPont moved the Highland Mine onto the former federal lands of Camp Blanding. In addition to ilmenite, other minerals were found in both mine locations, the most important of which were staurolite and zircon..

Under P.L. 493 and the agreement with the federal government, royalties from the Highland Mine were divided equally between the Armory Board and the federal government. Royalties on the Trail Ridge Mine continued to go entirely to the Armory Board. However, in August 1964 DuPont determined it had completely mined out the Trail Ridge tract on state lands. Mining then moved to former federal lands. This meant that all mining royalties would be divided equally between the Armory Board and the federal government and presented a serious financial management problem for the Armory Board.

Improvements to Camp Blanding, also required under the agreement with the federal government, continued with construction of an office for the state maintenance officer (who was also the post commander) and his staff, a $167,000 addition to the Combined Field Maintenance Shop, and a new building for Organizational Maintenance Shop No. 7.

In the biennium 1959—1960 the Armory Board renamed Sand Hill Lake "Lowry Lake" in honor of retired Lt Gen Sumter L. Lowry and named the known distance rifle ranges "Hutchison Range" in honor of retired Lt. Gen. Joseph C. Hutchison.

The next biennium, 1961—1962 saw some increased use of Camp Blanding. In addition to performing the higher echelon maintenance required on all federal equipment, the Combined Field Maintenance Shop at Camp Blanding was assigned the field maintenance mission for all vehicles and generators of Headquarters, United States Strike Command (now United States Central Command), MacDill Air Force Base. This contract was negotiated by Harry M. Hatcher who was then a lieutenant colonel and supervisor of the Field Maintenance Shop.

During the same biennium, an Officer Candidate School was established at Camp Blanding. Buildings were completely renovated for exclusive use of the school, including a headquarters and classroom building, two classrooms and study hall buildings, five barracks, a mess hall and a latrine.

Twenty other World War II frame buildings were salvaged and removed as no longer usable. Contract was let for $83,834 to renovate and join together three existing motor storage buildings for use as the USP & FO warehouse. Federal funds were provided for this project.

If the years beginning in 1955 represented a rebirth of Camp Blanding, the year 1965 marked a second coming of age for the post.

After about twenty years of far less than capacity use of Camp Blanding for Florida National Guard training, the years beginning in 1965 saw steadily increasing use.

THE NEW CAMP BLANDING

The Adjutant General's report for the years 1965 and 1966 recorded extensive use of Camp Blanding for various types of training. The Florida National Guard used the rifle, pistol and machine gun ranges for 37,616 man-days. At this time some units were designated for enhanced training in anticipation of possible federal mobilization for the war in VietNam. This training took place at Camp Blanding.

Another innovation was a Jungle Warfare Training site which became available in 1965. In that year elements of the entire 20th Special Forces Group from four states completed their Annual Field Training at Camp Blanding, and in 1966 Company C, 20th Special Forces Group, Florida National Guard, conducted two weeks of Military Occupational Specialty (MOS) training at Camp Blanding for personnel of all four states. In addition, 500 Guardsmen completed their required quarterly jumps on the Camp Blanding Drop Zones.

The Florida National Guard Officer Candidate School used post facilities for field training and graduated fifty-four new lieutenants in 1965 and seventy-nine in 1966.

In still another major development in expanded use of Camp Blanding, the 260th Engineer Group (Cbt), 261st Engineer Battalion (Cbt), 269th Engineer Company (Dp Trk), 314th Ordnance Company (GAS)and an element of the 181st Military Police Company joined forces for their two week Annual Field Training. This was an additional 11,000 man-days of training use of the post.

Regular and reserve forces of other services continued to use Camp Blanding for another 22,457 man-days of training.

To support these activities, federal training site funds were provided to repair the field house to include an auditorium and indoor training space. In addition, renovation work was accomplished on barracks, mess halls and latrines.

The Camp Blanding Management Fund which continued to derive its income from sale of timber products and mining royalties, was able to provide $75,171 in 1965 and $63,915 in 1966 for salaries and other operating expenses at Camp Blanding.

With United States involvement in the Vietnam War increasing, some National Guard and Reserve units were designated for enhanced training. Much of this was accomplished through extra weekend training sessions at Camp Blanding. The Adjutant General noted in his report for 1967 and 1968 that Camp Blanding reached its peak period since World War II with 55,701 man-days utilized in weekend training sessions. Annual Field Training represented another 146,868 man-days of training.

A 1967 incident that re-established Camp Blanding as the Florida National Guard annual training site was vividly described by Lt. Col. Sayer L. Frisbie IV in a research paper for the United States Army Command and General Staff College in 1979. He wrote "The advance detachment for Annual Field Training of 1967 already had arrived at Fort Stewart, GA, to prepare for the arrival of the Florida National Guard when

Governor Claude R. Kirk ordered the Guard to spend its encampment at Camp Blanding. Civil disturbances were becoming increasingly common during the 'long hot summer' of 1967, and Governor Kirk said he wanted the Guard (in its capacity as the state militia) close at hand in the event of riots in Florida."

The precaution turned out to be unnecessary, but it set a precedent that led to Camp Blanding's role through the ensuing years and continuing today as the primary training site for the Florida National Guard.

Continuing his account, Lt. Col. Frisbie recounted "During that first major encampment, most troops were housed in squad (general purpose, medium) tents on land from which basic trainee housing had been cleared two decades earlier. These battalion-sized areas were designated as Administrative Bivouac Areas A through E plus the company-sized AVCO (Aviation Company) area adjacent to the airfield. A decision was made to continue holding Florida National Guard Annual Training at Camp Blanding (with the exception of Field Artillery units, for which there were no adequate ranges at that time, and various specialized units which needed facilities not available at Camp Blanding).

"A five-year development plan was begun under the leadership of Maj. Gen. Henry W. McMillan, The Adjutant General. The primary thrust of the five-year plan was construction of permanent troop housing for a five-battalion brigade. Administrative Bivouac Areas A through E and the AVCO area were selected as the sites for permanent housing. Areas A through E were designed to accommodate a battalion each, with a battalion headquarters facility, company headquarters, supply and mess hall buildings, and barracks and latrines. The AVCO area was designed to accommodate an aviation company. A number of additional barracks buildings were erected in the original cantonment area."

Beginning in 1969 the Adjutant General's formal report to the governor became an annual report. Previously these reports had covered two years. In 1969 training facilities at Camp Blanding were enhanced considerably with completion of a new Antiaircraft Artillery Range, 81 mm and 4.2" mortar ranges, recoilless rifle range, construction of additional small arms ranges and expansion of tactical training and maneuver areas and tracked vehicle driving range. A post medical facility was established, logistical facilities and training quarters were improved with showers and latrines available for both weekend training and annual field training.

A notable achievement in 1969 was acquisition of a post chapel. All the World War II chapels had been torn down, and Maj. Gen. Henry W. McMillan, the Adjutant General, was eager to get a chapel on the post at Camp Blanding. On drives to St. Augustine for staff meetings, Col Hatcher noticed the chapel at the old Green Cove Springs Naval Base was not being used. General McMillan asked Col Hatcher and Col Gilchrist, the state quartermaster, to inquire about the possibility of getting it for Camp Blanding. The reaction was favorable, and the chapel was donated by J. Louis Reynolds who had acquired it as part of the old Naval Base. It was moved in sections to its present location at Camp Blanding. Chaplain (Major General) Francis L. Sampson, Chief of Chaplains, United States Army, provided the organ, pews and other furnishings, all of which made the chapel appropriate for use by all faiths and denominations. D. R. Hassfurder, Superintendent of Florida state prison at Raiford, assisted in landscaping the chapel grounds, and Major Rita M. Danielski, WAC, obtained donations of religious articles. The chapel was dedicated April 5, 1970 with Catholic, Protestant and Jewish chaplains participating. It was named Reynolds Chapel in honor of its donor.

THE DECADE OF THE 1970s

The decade of the 1970s saw steadily increasing use of Camp Blanding for training. Every year of the decade more than 20,000 man-days of weekend training were conducted, along with nearly 100,000 man-days of annual training by Florida National Guard plus another 20,000 man-days or more by regular and reserve troops of the army and the other services.

The same decade saw continued construction, building renovation and enhancement of training facilities. Utilizing federal funds, the Annual Training Equipment Pool maintenance building was completed and occupied in 1971.

The organizational structure at Camp Blanding was modified from time to time to meet the needs of the logistical support operations and of the units training there. A Headquarters Detachment, Camp Blanding, was formed in 1969. Col Harry M. Hatcher, Supervisor of the Ordnance Shops, was reassigned as post commander and camp site supervisor on a full-time basis. Effective 1 July 1971, Headquarters Detachment, Camp Blanding, was reorganized as the 653rd Engineer Detachment, Army National Guard Training Site.

In 1973 Colonel Hatcher was reassigned as state maintenance officer upon the retirement of Colonel James A. Griffin. At this time Colonel Fred Lewellen became post commander.

All the logistical support functions continued throughout the decade at an increasing tempo to meet the needs of increasing numbers of troops training at Camp Blanding, both on weekends and for annual training.

Despite increased military use, Camp Blanding continued to assist the surrounding civilian community. A ninety-acre tract was made available to the Gateway Girl Scout Council for camping and other activities of youth groups. As many as 3,000 Girl Scouts used the camping facilities on occasion.

Beginning in 1973 the federal government funded a long-range construction program at Camp Blanding to provide permanent type barracks, latrines, mess halls and administrative buildings. This program was completed in five phases as follows:

Phase I (1974)	11 buildings	$ 406,336
Phase II (1975)	17 buildings	498,454
Phase III (1976)	54 buildings	1,919,880
Phase IV (1977)	38 buildings	1,394,998
Phase V (1977)	34 buildings	1,321,821

The Camp Blanding Sewage Treatment Plant was modernized in 1978 at a cost of $303,275, utilizing federal funds. A new post, camp or station warehouse building was completed in 1979 replacing the old Field House, which burned totally in October 1977. This cost $481,000. Funds came from the Florida Fire Insurance Trust Fund. A new Service Club was erected in 1980 on the site of the old Enlisted Men's Club ,which burned in December 1978. With 8,000 square feet, this facility cost $248,091. By the end of the decade of the 1970s, the reported value of buildings at Camp Blanding had reached $5,000,000.

For Army Aviation training at Camp Blanding, Nap-of-the-Earth (NOE) training courses were selected and surveyed and a Program of Instruction prepared and approved by First United States Army and the National Guard Bureau. NOE qualification training provides the aviators skills necessary in various modes of terrain flight in a Mid to High Intensity Battlefield.

The Florida National Guard Officer Candidate School was reorganized and redesignated the Florida National Guard Military Academy effective September 1, 1975, when a Florida National Guard Noncommissioned Officer School was established as part of the academy. The program included 113 hours of academic and leadership instruction.

Army Aviation units were routinely conducting training at Camp Blanding as were Special Forces troops, using facilities tailored to meet their requirements.

Camp Blanding was honored in 1995 as an army-wide "Community of Excellence", and the award was accepted by Lt. Col. Norman L. Redding (center), Training Site Manager/ Deputy Post Commander.

Infantry troops on a training exercise today, led by Maj. Gen. Ronald Harrison, the Adjutant General of Florida. (squatting)

The Light Antitank Weapon (LAW) on one of the Camp Blanding ranges today.

THE DECADE OF THE 1980s

After a decade notable for new building construction, modernization of facilities and increased tempo of training, the next decade saw still further increased training and construction to meet the needs of the troops. Regular Army troops, National Guard units of other states and Army Reserve troops made increased use of Camp Blanding's excellent facilities.

A major new project beginning in 1980 was an armory and post headquarters Building at Camp Blanding. The original design in 1980 was for 38,300 square feet estimated to cost $2,100,000. Because of unit reorganizations, some re-design of the building was required.

The structure was completed in 1984 with 35,441 square feet at a cost of $1,747,101. The project included renovation of the World War II era post hospital fountain, still in its original location which is now the main entrance to this facility. In moments of levity Col Harry Hatcher claims ownership of the fountain because it was listed as part of the hospital purchased by him and his father in 1947. In 1986 a Conference/Briefing Room was completed with audio-visual equipment including closed circuit TV, video projection and voice activated sound system. The cost was $237,390. Occupation of this modern post headquarters facility culminated a series of moves and provided the capability for command and control for current missions and for any future expansion. During World War II, post headquarters was located on A Road just south of Quarters 1 which was the post commander's house during the war. In 1969 post headquarters was located in the south end of what is now the post exchange building. From 1970 to 1984 headquarters was in a regimental headquarters building on the northwest side of the parade ground, a building now used by the Military Academy.

Effective October 1, 1984, the Installation Support Unit was activated as the command structure for Camp Blanding, reporting directly to The Adjutant General. The 653rd Engineer Detachment continued as a separate unit.

A new Telephone Exchange Building was completed in 1981 at a cost of $60,990 in federal funds. Underground telephone wiring systems had been installed over the past two years by a unit of the Georgia Air National Guard and the 146th Signal Battalion utilizing weekend and annual training periods.

Rehabilitation of four mess halls was completed in time for most 1982 Annual Training periods. The cost was $153,000 in federal funds. Rehabilitation of the Overhead Electrical Distribution System was completed in 1982 at a cost of $3,000, also with 100 percent federal funds.

In 1983, the Field Artillery Range was activated with the addition of three mounds to provide observation posts at heights of forty, fifty and sixty-feet at a cost of $172,124 in federal funds.

Construction projects for the Florida Air National Guard also continued. Projects completed in Fiscal Year 1986—1987 included construction of new facilities and renovation of temporary facilities on the post at a cost of $358,000. Another project that year was preparation of a master plan for permanent facilities.

Eleven other construction projects for the Army National Guard were at various stages of design, the largest of which were a Brigade Headquarters Complex budgeted at $1,429,000 and the Florida Military Academy expansion budgeted at $1,224,000.

The Adjutant General's report for FY 1987—1988 showed 15 construction projects at various stages of development. Expansion of the Mobilization and Training Equipment Site was completed at a cost of $1,175,337. Approximately $3,350,000 in federal funds were obligated for Air National Guard construction projects and approximately $3,345,000 in additional projects were under design.

The largest single project under construction at Camp Blanding that year was the Regional Training Site-Maintenance (RTS-M) at a cost of $1,877,500. The RTS-M was organized to provide sustainment and transitional training for individuals on force modernization equipment. It was to serve both Army National Guard and Army Reserve personnel of Florida, Puerto Rico and the Virgin Islands with a staff of thirteen full-time Active Duty National Guard personnel (AGR).

By the end of the decade of the 1980s, Camp Blanding had 300 employees, and the value of buildings on the post was listed at $27,712,767 plus additional value of $1,747,101 for the post headquarters and armory building.

Training continued to expand at Camp Blanding with more than 350,000 man-days utilized during several years of the decade.

Income generated for the Camp Blanding Management Trust Fund from timber sales and mining royalties continued to increase in the decade of the 1980s. It reached $3,038,015 in the fiscal year 1989—1990, providing funds for salaries and other operating expenses of the post.

Special Forces unit training is offered today at Camp Blanding, not only for the Florida National Guard unit, but also for other units of the Army.

SUPPORT FOR DESERT STORM

In the Fall of 1990, Camp Blanding received a request from the 101st Airborne Division (Air Assault) for classified support in its deployment to Operation Desert Storm. The division needed a large area to stage its rotary wing aircraft, which would move through the Port of Jacksonville en route to the Middle East. Consultations with the post commander, operations group and airfield control resulted in approval of the request.

Under command of the assistant division commander, helicopters of the 101st flew from their home station at Fort Campbell, KY, to Camp Blanding. Every landing zone on the post was used. At times more than 100 aircraft were dispersed all over the post awaiting clearance to move to the port in Jacksonville. During this staging operation, Camp Blanding fed the ground troops arriving in convoys and provided some maintenance support also.

This operation was a major accomplishment for Camp Blanding and was recognized as such by the 101st Airborne Division, which gave the post a Certificate of Appreciation.

Its after-action report noted importance of the use of Camp Blanding. This was incorporated into mobilization plans of the 101st Division and subsequently tested in mobilization exercises by the division.

A lazer range finder for artillery and aircraft bombs, on one of the many Camp Blanding ranges today.

DOWNSIZING IN THE 1990s

After so many years of build-up in United States military strength to deter aggression by the Soviet Union and the Warsaw Pact, the end of the "Cold War" brought downsizing throughout the Defense Department. This long, slow process of reorganizing military units, including the National Guard, is still going on as this book is written. Camp Blanding is affected by federal budget constraints, which make it more difficult to get appropriated funds for capital outlay as well as operation and maintenance accounts.

Construction and modernization reached a peak in 1992 when buildings at Camp Blanding were valued at $30,204,508. Other than federal appropriations, operations at Camp Blanding were funded by the Camp Blanding Management Trust Fund which continued to derive its income from mining royalties and timber sales. That fund provided $3,881,832 in expenditures in 1993.

Some important projects were undertaken or completed in the first half of the decade of the 1990s. Expansion of the Florida Military Academy was completed in 1993 at a cost of

$1,471,982. The biggest single new project undertaken in the 1990s was construction of a simulated city for training in Military Operations in Urban Terrain (MOUT). This project, now called Smithville, is now in use by both National Guard and regular Army troops.

But the year 1993 saw other developments, which produced severe financial problems for Camp Blanding. The red-cockade woodpecker, an endangered species, established nesting areas at several places within the post. Always sensitive to environmental considerations, Camp Blanding ceased logging operations to protect the safety of these woodpeckers. At about the same time the DuPont mining operations were curtailed. The result of these two developments was a severe reduction in cash flow to the Camp Blanding Management Trust Fund, which was the source of all state funding of post operation. The result was a severe cutback in full-time personnel.

For Fiscal Year 1995, expenditures of the Camp Blanding Management Trust Fund dropped to $948,500 from more than $3,000,000 per year in previous years. Federal funding continued for several important construction projects on the post including an aviation fuel facility, expansion of the bachelor officers quarters (Finnegan Lodge), the MOUT training facility referred to above and a Light Anti-Armor Weapons (LAW) Range. A major new project was undertaken to construct a storage facility for solid rocket motors being used at the Kennedy Space Center, Cape Canaveral, FL. This project will provide income for the Camp Blanding Management Trust Fund as will major training exercises conducted at Camp Blanding by CENTCOM for United States world-wide forces.

Initiatives like these, along with strict financial management, are helping to sustain current operations at Camp Blanding for the Florida National Guard, regular and reserve forces of all services and units and individuals of allied nations.

CAMP BLANDING TODAY

Today Camp Blanding is owned by the state of Florida and operated by the Department of Military Affairs, Florida National Guard. Management of the Camp Blanding Training Site is vested in the Installation Support Unit (ISU), a major command of the Florida Army National Guard. The ISU has a strength of 222 Guardsmen, ninety-four state employees and thirty-four federal employees.

As this book is written the Camp Blanding commander is Colonel Jerry Neff. The full-time training site manager/ deputy post commander is Lt. Col. Norman L. Redding.

Florida Army National Guard units stationed at Camp Blanding as part of the ISU are the 221st Ordnance Detachment with a strength of twenty-five; 253rd Medical Detachment with a strength of twenty-three, and 653rd Engineer Detachment with a strength of sixty-four. Also part of the ISU is the 269th Engineer Company stationed at Live Oak. Other units stationed at Camp Blanding are the 320th Special Forces Battalion; Headquarters and Headquarters Detachment, 927th Corps Support Battalion; the 850rd Quartermaster

Company; 464th Ordnance Company, and the Regional Train-
ing Site-Maintenance (discussed elsewhere in this book).
Other significant activities on Camp Blanding are the Mili-
tary Academy, recently re-designated the Regional Training
Institute, Florida; Combined Maintenance Shops; Director of
Logistics warehouse and other logistical support elements.

The current mission assigned to the Camp Blanding Training Site follows:

> To prepare to activate mobilization operations
> in order to receive and support designated
> units for federal and state missions, and pro-
> vide administrative services, training and logis-
> tical support to state and federal agencies, both
> military and civilian.

The Air National Guard 202nd Red Horse Civil Engineering Squadron with a strength of 207 is stationed at Camp
Blanding with the following mission:

> The unit is a highly mobile, rapidly deployable
> civil engineering response force that is self-suf-
> ficient for limited periods of time. It is capable
> of performing heavy damage repair required
> for the recovery of critical Air Force facilities
> and utility systems required for aircraft launch
> and recovery, which have been subject to en-
> emy attack or natural disaster. In peacetime,
> the unit acts as an engineering response force
> that can support special operations and
> contingencies.

Two other Air National Guard units are stationed at Camp
Blanding. The 159th Weather Flight with a strength of twenty-
one has a wartime mission to provide meteorological services
and weather forecasting to the Air Force and the Army. The
Air National Guard Weather Readiness Training Center at Camp

Blanding provides basic and intermediate level training for Air National Guard Weather Flights throughout the country.

The economic impact of the Camp Blanding Training Site on the local community in 1995, including federal and state expenditures, was $11,059,495. The economic impact of the Air National Guard units at Camp Blanding was an additional $3,051,900. The value of the facilities total more than $40,000,000.

Despite budget constraints which show no signs of abating in the foreseeable future, Camp Blanding is alive and well— able to accomplish its mission today and prepared to expand if required to meet future federal or state requirements.

Although Camp Blanding is not widely known in the civilian world, it is recognized throughout the military establishment for its outstanding ranges, training facilities and dedicated support capability. All these facilities are being utilized today on a regular basis. The training support and facilities are used by varying size units from squad/section to and including a separate infantry brigade, an artillery brigade, an attack helicopter battalion, and special operations forces from one team to several companies or a battalion. These organizations conduct various individual weapons and crew served firing and qualifications, field training exercises and live fire exercises up to brigade level, and combined arms live fire exercises incorporating small arms, crew served weapons, artillery, mortars and aerial delivery weapons systems. Additionally, command post exercises; land navigation; maneuver; special operations training, including airborne (parachute) operations; and limited amphibious operations are supported.

The Camp Blanding Training Site has thirty-five surveyed artillery firing positions with three earthen constructed observation points. The firing positions are adequate for 105 mm, 155 mm and 8" artillery. The installation has an Aerial Gunnery Range, which accommodates rocket firing, mini-gun firing for attack helicopters and door gunnery firing for lift helicopters. There are several Forward Area Refueling Rearming points. The aerial gunnery impact area will also accommodate fires from all weapons systems associated with the AC-130 Gunship and most weapon systems associated with fixed wing aircraft using inert warheads. Thirty-seven tactical mortar firing points capable of firing 81 mm, 60 mm, 107 mm and 120 mm mortars are available for training.

Simulator Training Aids

With budgetary constraints and downsizing of the army, Camp Blanding sought ways to continue providing support for all units and personnel training on the post. Simulation devices were determined to be a major method of accomplishing this goal. Representatives of the post visited other Army and Air Force installations, which had simulation devices of various kinds. Camp Blanding then developed a Simulation Center by installing climate control in an existing warehouse to accommodate the required computers.

This Simulation Center provides a facility for computer-driven command post exercises at battalion level or higher. Units can use their own computers and programs with subordinate units in outside tentage or connect to the power system and computer program inside the Center. Several scenarios are available. The enhanced infantry brigade of the Florida National Guard has used this facility. Plans now are to expand it to accommodate units larger than brigade.

In addition, the Center includes an Engagement Skills facility. An infantry squad of twelve men can be tested on their reactions to enemy attacks. The system includes the sounds of weapons fired by the enemy and by the tested squad. After the exercise, the results are provided for the squad and each member.

CENTCOM Worldwide Exercise

United States Central Command (CENTCOM), a unified command stationed at MacDill Air Force Base, conducted a major worldwide training exercise at Camp Blanding in April 1996, utilizing extensive facilities of the post under contract with the Florida National Guard. Post headquarters became CENTCOM Headquarters for this exercise. More than thirty general and flag officers participated. Most of them were quartered in Finnegan Lodge on the post.

This exercise provided a valuable learning experience for the Camp Blanding staff. It was the first instance of the use of Camp Blanding for a major joint force exercise.

So pleased were CENTCOM commanders that future exercises at Camp Blanding are being considered.

Urban Terrain Training Site

On a thirty-acre site within Camp Blanding sits a mock city of concrete block buildings. Popularly known as Smithville, its purpose is to provide training for army troops in Military Operations in Urban Terrain (MOUT). Completed in 1994 at a cost of $2.2 million dollars, mostly in federal funds, it provides realism in the kind of urban combat likely in any future war. It is one of only three in the nation large enough to train an entire battalion.

Observing the training in March 1995, Marcia Goodge, a reporter for the *Bradford Telegraph*, described it this way:

> People strolled in the streets of the sleepy vil-
> lage of Smithville off SR-21 on Camp Blanding
> property. Men, women and children carried on
> everyday activity—until the quiet was broken by
> an explosion that rocked the town. Mortars im-

pacted on the roads and sidewalks, pouring multi-colored smoke into the air. The smoke masked the rapid advance of the attacking troops as they circumnavigated trenches and machine gun nests....The attackers readied themselves to sweep through the town, taking over each building one by one while rifle fire stuttered and grenades boomed.

The MOUT facility has been used not only by the Florida National Guard but also by the 82nd Airborne Division and by a battalion of the Royal Canadian Army. Other United States and foreign troops will be using this facility because of its size, convenience and availability of support facilities at Camp Blanding.

MOBILE ASPHALT PRODUCTION PLANT

In 1994 Camp Blanding became the home of the United States military's second mobile asphalt production plant. This $1.8 million facility can produce 180 tons of asphalt per hour, is completely computerized and can be broken down and moved within forty-eight hours.

First use of the plant at Camp Blanding was to build roads. This environmentally friendly facility can be operated by three technicians. It enhances training of engineer units. Normal turnaround time per truck for commercial manufacturers is four hours. Camp Blanding and the Florida National Guard can produce its own asphalt at a significant cost saving.

SOLID ROCKET STORAGE FACILITY

Beating out other bidders in 1994, Camp Blanding was selected by the U.S. Air Force as the storage site for solid rocket motors used in Titan IV space launch vehicles at Cape Canaveral. The twenty-eight million facility will be used by Martin Marietta Corporation. Part of the project cost will be used to improve rail access to Camp Blanding. This provides a collateral benefit to units training at Camp Blanding.

LIGHTNING DAMAGE STUDY PROJECT

The University of Florida and the Florida National Guard are collaborating in a major study of lightning damage, seeking methods of reducing damage to electronic equipment such as radar as well as human life. The project is located on Camp Blanding which lies in an area particularly susceptible to lightning strikes.

University of Florida Professor Martin Uman, one of the world's leading experts on lightning, notes that much more information is needed about how lightning starts and how it attaches to the ground. The project at Camp Blanding has an extensive array of overhead wires to which lightning is attracted by sending a small rocket into the air trailed by a strand of copper wire when lightning seems imminent. Scientists of several other countries are participating.

RECREATION FACILITIES

Camp Blanding today provides extensive recreation facilities for military personnel and their families. Trailers and quonset huts near the lake are available for rentals, as well as camping and picnic facilities and space for recreational vehicles. Equipment is also available through the Morale, Welfare and Recreation Department. Widely used by National Guard personnel and their families, these facilities are a significant recruiting tool for the Florida National Guard.

ENVIRONMENTAL PROTECTION

Ecosystems on Camp Blanding include pine forests, hardwoods, oak scrub, cypress swamps, springs, creeks and lakes. The Florida Army National Guard natural resource managers are working to conserve and restore these systems to benefit all of Camp Blanding's plants and animals.

Environmental activities at Camp Blanding have been successful because they have involved all concerned government and private interests. In 1993 Brig. Gen. Richard Capps, Assistant Adjutant General, brought together environmentalists from the University of Florida, United States Fish and Wildlife Service and other government and private groups to develop jointly an Integrated Natural Resources Management Plan to address training needs, revenue-generating land uses such as forestry, the protection of threatened species, habitat restoration programs, water resources management, recreation activities and regional wildlife implications.

The red-cockaded woodpecker is only one of many species at Camp Blanding needing protection and nurturing. They are getting it through this program in ways, which do not interfere with the training mission of Camp Blanding.

Community of Excellence Award

For the year 1995 Camp Blanding was runner-up installation in the army-wide competition as a Community of Excellence. All army installations—Active, Reserve and National Guard—compete on the basis of effective and efficient services rendered to all who use its facilities and to its nearby civilian communities. The criteria are strictly scored by Department of the Army inspection teams.

Camp Blanding placed first among small installations army-wide and received a cash award of $25,000 and a plaque for display in post headquarters. The award was accepted in a ceremony by Col. Neff and Lt. Col. Redding.

Visitors to the Camp Blanding Museum today can see exhibits depicting what the post was like more than fifty years ago and at the same time see evidence of the forward-looking approach of today.

APPENDICES

CAMP BLANDING MUSEUM

As early as 1980 a group of Florida National Guard members conceived the idea of a World War II Museum at Camp Blanding. Credit for this idea goes to the Florida National Guard as an institution, not to any single individual. The idea was timely because the fiftieth anniversary of World War II was approaching, and national plans were developing to commemorate major events of that war which unified the nation to preserve the freedoms we all enjoy today.

The Florida National Guard saw the proposed museum and Memorial Park as a method of telling the important story of World War II to a wide audience, especially young people. Its appeal would also be to community leaders, educators and members of the National Guard family. Survey after survey shows high school and college students fail to understand the events of World War II or their impact on the lives of everyone living today. The museum project had the full support of The Adjutant General Maj. Gen. Robert F. Ensslin, Jr., and continues to have the support of his successor Maj. Gen. Ronald O. Harrison.

Plans for the museum were drawn by a team including Col. Carl Swindull, Chief of Staff of the Florida National Guard; Lt. Col .Kent Petelle, Training Site Manager at Camp Blanding; Robert Hawk, Florida National Guard Historian; CSM Rodney

Hall, who became the museum director, and SGM James F. Bloodworth, who became the first president of the Camp Blanding Museum and Historical Association. Their blueprint was approved by The Adjutant General of Florida in the form of a master plan which provided details of the site plan, funding, command and control, Initial funds were appropriated by the State Legislature based on this master plan, effective July 1, 1989.

Rodney Hall became director of the museum, and work progressed rapidly with the help of a large number of enthusiastic volunteers including many current members of the National Guard. The museum project consisted of three major parts:

THE MUSEUM. An old World War II Guest House (barracks-type building) immediately inside the Main Gate off S.R. 16 was converted to the museum. After ridding the building of asbestos, termites, mice and feral cats, the inside was reconstructed to meet the needs of the museum. Downstairs became the public display area with sections for each of the nine "Blanding Divisions," an area for the 508th Parachute Infantry and space for artifacts from all the activities at Camp Blanding, including the Infantry Replacement Training Center. A small gift shop is also on the first floor. The second floor provides storage space, offices, the archives, workroom and a large conference room.

THE FLORIDA REGIMENTAL MEMORIAL. Space adjacent to the museum was allocated to a memorial to the Florida National Guard participation in World War II. Its dominating feature is a fifteen-foot statue of an infantry soldier. It includes a wall displaying maps of the combat areas of major Florida National Guard units in World War II. A tablet of stone carries names of mobilized members who were killed in action. This area is the site of almost all the public events staged by the museum.

THE MEMORIAL PARK. A thirteen-acre area provides space for display of large artifacts such as tanks, trucks, aircraft and weapons. Within the Memorial Park a section was set aside for each

"Blanding Division" to erect its own monument. Veterans organizations of all the divisions were contacted. Without exception all nine divisions designed and paid for their own monuments in their assigned areas. Veterans of the 508th Parachute Infantry, which had already sponsored a monument on the post, gave the project enthusiastic support. The Florida National Guard secured a C-47 aircraft for display beside the 508th monument. The plane, produced in 1941, is the kind from which the 508th jumped into Normandy. Additionally monuments were erected honoring Medal of Honor holders, Purple Heart holders, American Prisoners of War and the Infantry Replacement Training Center. The Military Order of the World Wars erected a monument honoring "all who served."

Part of the master plan contemplated organization of a non-profit association with the sole mission of supporting the museum by providing volunteers and assisting in other ways, particularly in communicating with veterans and other groups and in staging public events at the museum.

Accordingly, the Camp Blanding Museum and Historical Associates, Inc., a Florida non-profit corporation, was formally organized at a meeting at Camp Blanding April 1, 1989. James F. Bloodworth was elected its first president for a two-year term as provided in bylaws, which were adopted at the meeting.

With its documentation in order, the corporation was granted tax-exempt status by the Internal Revenue Service, which made it eligible to receive tax-deductible contributions. Memberships were solicited principally among veterans, but anyone interested in the objectives of the museum is eligible to join. Contributions were invited, and the association assembled a modest fund. Officers and directors receive no compensation or reimbursement of travel expenses. The Board of approximately twenty members meets quarterly.

The first major task of the association was to plan and organize dedication of the museum. An association Planning Committee worked for more than a year to plan every detail of the dedication ceremony. That event on November 25, 1990, the fiftieth anniversary of mobilization of the Florida National Guard for World War II, drew an audience of 3,000. Lieutenant General Robert Arter, director of the national World War II Commemoration Committee, was the dedication speaker.

The Camp Blanding Museum became a major participant in the national commemoration program with the association arranging frequent programs to which the public was invited. As a result of this activity, Camp Blanding was designated a national Commemorative Community. Lieutenant General C.M. Kicklighter, who succeeded General Arter as Executive Director of the Commemoration Committee, presented a World War II Commemorative flag to the Camp Blanding commander in a ceremony at the museum Oct. 24, 1992.

While the fiftieth anniversary commemoration continued, the Camp Blanding Museum and Historical Association developed an expansion plan to honor veterans of conflicts since World War II—namely, Korea, Vietnam and Desert Storm— and to preserve the museum project in perpetuity. The State Armory Board approved this plan August 28, 1993 and allocated an additional thirteen acres for the expansion.

The Vietnam Veterans of North Florida volunteered to serve as the action organization to develop the Vietnam area. Their plan envisions a model Fire Base with features typical of the various types of fire bases used in Vietnam. That section was dedicated in a ceremony April 29, 1995.

Carson Kirk, of Dacula, Georgia, an early visitor to the museum, recorded his emotions and expressed the spirit of the museum project eloquently in a newspaper column published by the Powell Valley News, Pennington Gap, Virginia, December 2, 1992, reproduced with permission on pages 201-202.

CAMP BLANDING MEMORIES
By: Carson Kirk

Heading home from Florida in March 1992, decided to drive by Camp Blanding near Starke, FL. It was never open to the public for the twelve years I lived in Florida, but to my surprise it was open. The guard at the gate said, "drive around as much as you want, just don't cross the railroad anywhere on the base, and don't take pictures of the training facilities."

They opened a museum just over a year ago just inside the main gate. The thousands that went through basic training plus every division that trained there is well represented by the museum.

After touring the museum we drove around the base. Nothing looked very familiar, the old huts had been replaced with more modern barracks. The old guest house and the generals house were the only ones left standing from my days there almost fifty years ago.

Kingsley Lake looked the same, how well I remember the five mile speed marches around it before daybreak. The Florida National Guard is based there, but at this time of year there were very few soldiers on base and just an occasional Army vehicle passing by.

I got out of the car and looked out over the land as level as a table top, dotted with pines, palms and grass growing about as well as it can in the sandy soil. The white sand is still hard to look at in the bright sunshine.

I looked out across the railroad, where the guard said not to go, out beyond the scrub oak, pines and under brush, out there I think in that direction lies Mud Lake, swamps, mosquitoes and wild hogs. Out there, and now all around me are the memories. Memories of the place teeming with young soldiers, the most were like myself, away from home for the first time, and for many a short furlough home after basic training then on into combat and for some never to return again.

As I stood there I could hear the voices, the fast clipped speech of North and East, a Midwestern farm boys half drawl and the pure Southern drawl. Laughter, curses, banter and always the complaining. All around me I could see the faces, hundreds of them, Captain Rayburn. Lt. Bennett, Lt. Price and First Sgt. Leatherwood, how that name fit him, his skin looked like leather baked under the Florida sun.

Just across the railroad standing in a patch of white sand were the boys from Lee County, VA. Here's the ones I recognized— my cousin Hayes Kirk, Clarence Napier, Jack Evans, Carl Kegley, Calvin parsons, David Gillenwater, Elmer Neeley, another cousin Clyde Rhea and the smiling face of Charles Goins. As I looked at the young faces from almost fifty years ago I thought, where are they now?

My cousin Hayes is in a nursing home in Big Stone Gap, VA. I went to see him, he didn't talk and only opened his eyes twice, so I don't know if he recognized me. Clarence was like a brother to me in our young days and that hasn't changed. The feeling is still there. Jack and Carl died a few years ago, I have lost touch with Calvin and Elmer. David was in bad health that last time I saw him. My other cousin Clyde was wounded in battle and lost the use of one arm, he died about ten year ago.

As I watched them a crow was calling from a nearby pine tree, and out there somewhere in the swamps I could hear a bugle clear as day, someone was playing taps. I turned toward the sound for a few seconds and when I looked again at the patch of sand they were all gone except for Charles, he stood there smiling.

The bright sun shining on the white sand caused my eyes to fill with tears and I had to turn away, for you see, Charles never returned home to the hills of Lee County again. Our Troopship was torpedoed in the English Channel and the channel became his grave.

So to all the men who trained at Camp Blanding, in my mind I heard and saw some of you there in March of 1992. The bugle sounded for some of you in the war and many have died since.

And for those of us remaining the youth has faded from our faces long ago and the sound is ever closer. Maybe that's why I heard it so clear coming out of the swamps of Camp Blanding. God bless all of you and lets hope Camp Blanding forever remains a shrine to the young men who trained there, and even a hundred years from now someone will see us standing in a patch of sand and will have to turn away with tears in their eyes from the bright sunshine.

ALBERT H. BLANDING

When Camp Blanding was built in 1939, it was named for Major General Albert H. Blanding on recommendation of the Florida National Guard Officers Association, approved by the State Armory Board and Governor Fred P. Cone. He served thirty-five years in the Florida National Guard, commanded the 31st Infantry Division and was Chief of the War Department National Guard Bureau 1936-1940.

General Blanding was born in Lyons, Iowa, November 9, 1876, died in Bartow, Florida, December 26, 1970, at the age of ninty-four. He moved to Florida in 1878 and graduated number one in his class from the East Florida Seminary (now University of Florida) in 1894.

He enlisted in the Gainesville Guards, Florida State Troops in 1895 and served in the enlisted ranks until its disbandment before the Spanish-American War. He was commissioned a captain in the Florida National Guard in 1899, serving first as adjutant of the 2nd Florida Infantry. He commanded the regiment on the Mexican Border in 1916—1917 displaying outstanding command ability.

In August 1917, Colonel Blanding was mustered into federal service and promoted to Brigadier General. He saw World War I action in many battles in France and Germany. He returned to the United States in 1919 and received the Distinguished Service Medal for his outstanding war record.

On October 15, 1924, General Blanding assumed command of the 31st Infantry Division and was promoted to Major General. In 1936 President Franklin D. Roosevelt appointed him Chief of the National Guard Bureau. He served with distinction in that position and retained command of the 31st Division until 1940. He retired from the Florida National Guard November 9, 1940, with rank of Lieutenant General, retired.

During World War II General Blanding was recalled to duty by Governor Spessard L. Holland to serve as Military Advisor to the governor and as Coordinating Director of action divisions of the State Defense Council. General Blanding is widely recognized as one of Florida's most outstanding military personalities.

ADJUTANTS GENERAL OF FLORIDA

Theodore W. Brevard	1861
William H. Milton	1861
Hugh Archer	1864
Horatio Jenkins, Jr.	Jul. 9, 1868—Aug. 4, 1868
George B. Carse	Aug. 5, 1868—Feb. 20, 1870
John Varnum	Feb. 21, 1870—Mar. 4, 1877
John J. Dickison	Mar. 5, 1877—Jan. 16, 1881
James E. Yonge	Jan. 17, 1881— Jan. 16, 1885
David Lang	Jan. 17, 1885—Dec. 4, 1893
Patrick Houstoun	Dec. 5, 1893— May 6, 1901
William A. MacWilliams (resigned)	May 7, 1901—Jun. 28, 1901
J. Clifford R. Foster	Jun. 29, 1901— Jan. 9, 1917
J. B. Christian	Jan. 10, 1917—Mar. 29, 1919
James McCants	Mar. 30, 1919—Aug. 31, 1919
Sidney J. Catts, Jr.	Sept. 1, 1919—Jan. 3, 1921
Charles P. Lovell	Jan. 4, 1921—Jan. 25, 1923
J. Clifford R. Foster	Feb. 23, 1923—Jun. 18, 1928
Vivian Collins	Jun. 29, 1928—Apr. 15, 1947
Mark W. Lance	Apr. 16, 1947—Apr. 27, 1962
Henry W. McMillan	Apr. 28, 1962—Aug. 12, 1975

Kennedy C. Bullard   Aug. 13, 1975—Dec. 31, 1981
Robert F. Ensslin, Jr.   Jan. 1, 1982—Feb. 28, 1992
Ronald O. Harrison   Mar. 1, 1992—to date

CAMP BLANDING COMMANDERS

WORLD WAR II COMMANDERS:

Maj R. R. Reynolds   Sept. 14, 1940—

Col R. H. Kelley

Maj Gen John J. Persons
(Commander, 31st Division)

Maj Gen Morris B. Payne
(Commander, 43rd Division)

Brig Gen L. A. Kunzig   Jul. 15, 1941—Dec. 31, 1943
(first Army Service Forces commander)

Col Walter E. Smith   Jan. 1, 1944—Jun. 21, 1944

Col Edward C. Rose   Jun. 21, 1944—Jun. 30, 1945.

Brig. Gen. Robert S. Israel, Jr.   Jul. 1, 1945—

POST-WAR COMMANDERS:

Col James A. Griffin
Col Harry M. Hatcher Jr.
Col Fred A. Lewellen
Col Augustin Gonzalez
Col James C. Rinaman
Col James F. Campbell, Jr.
Col Leo A. Lorenzo
Col James E. Rogers, Jr.
Col Kent R. Petelle
Col Frederic J. Raymond
Col. Jerry L. Neff

CEMETERIES AT CAMP BLANDING

When land was acquired for construction of Camp Blanding in 1939—1940, it included four known civilian cemeteries associated with churches or congregations. All are still in existence, marked and fenced. In addition, a German Prisoner of War cemetery was established for burial of seven German prisoners who died while stationed at Camp Blanding.

At least two surveys have been made, the most recent in 1987, to verify exact location, size and condition of the cemeteries. Wherever possible names of individuals interred have been recorded and are included in this appendix.

The largest of the civilian cemeteries is the Beulah cemetery. The Beulah Missionary Baptist Church, erected before the Civil War, was moved from the campsite to its present location on Florida State Road 21 west of Camp Blanding. The church still exists today, and its members have been given permission to visit and maintain the cemetery.

During the 1987 survey one additional cemetery was located, apparently a family burial ground with only three graves bearing the name Conway. Thus cemeteries now on Camp Blanding total six—five civilian plus the German POW cemetery, Information from the 1987 survey included the following data: location by coordinates on Camp Blanding Special Map Series V7475, directions to site, size of cemetery, number of graves and names of those interred wherever possible.

BEULAH CEMETERY

Location: Coordinates 11351240. Beulah Cemetery is identified on the map. It is located 50 meters northwest of the dirt road intersection at 11401235.

Size: 125 by 50 meters.

Grave sites: 102.

Names on the markers:

Leland Boree	Melvin Boree
L. R. Britt	Rachel Bonnette
Leon Bonnett	Winnie H. Boree
Genie Britt	Jas. Burney
L.Z. Conway	Eld C. Conway
Infant Daughter(Conway)	Infant Son Charles (Conway)
Alva Mae Conway	James G. Conway
K.B. Drew	Mary Drew
Martha Drew	James M. Drew
Eugene Gnann	Thomas F. Harris
Nannie Harris	Leonard C. Harris
Ella E. Harris	Winnie Harris Boree
Patrick H. Harris	R.E. Jones
Theresa Jones	Jessee Weeks
Laura Lane Weeks	Rebecca Lane
Austin Thomas	Paul Thomas
Jesse Thomas	James O. Wilkinson
Mamie Weeks	Jesse Harris
Lilla Mae Sapp	Elsie Mae Sapp
James H. Sapp	Cab Harris
Clinton T. Harris	W.R. Harris
Mary Harris	Estelle Harris
William Richard Harris	Eugene W. Hickey
Lorena Hickey	Willliam D. Holder
Albert Holder	Mary Holder
Louise V. McCaffrey	Barbara Louise Miller
I.H.A. Morng	William J. Kersey
Percy Kersey	Ruby Kersey
Loyd T. Kersey	Leaman H. Kersey
Samuel Perry	Cornelia Perry
M.C. Saunders	Martha J. Spencer
Kenney Thomas	Minnie Thomas
Hattie V. Thomas	Mary F. Thomas

LaFayette Thomas   W.M. Thomas
Josephine Thomas   Louisa Thomas
Dola Thompson   Mary A. Tillis
James A. Weeks   Ethel Weeks
Iris Louise Weeks   Laura Evelyn Weeks
James M. Wilson   Mrs. Mary Wilson
Lee Roy Wilson   Mary M. Wilson
James H. Wilson   Mrs. Idella Wilson
James M. Wilson   William R. Wilson
Little Rosa Wilson   James E. Wilson

Graves listed in Record of Burials but not located during the survey:

E.W. Donnelly   Ellen M. Dowling
Ervin Higginbotham   Elizabeth Morgan
Jess F. Moody   James H. Sapp
Earnest Saunders   Maggie Saunders
Mary E. Thomas   Leonard M. Thomas
Elouise Thomas   Cullin Thomas
Elender Weeks   Martha J. Weeks
Lewis Weeks   Arabella Weeks
Jesse Wilson   Billy Underwood
Child of Crews Wainwright
Fanny Conway
Sallie Conway Wilson   Lewis Wilson
Nancy Wilson   Henry Clay Priest
Louise Rooks Priest   Infant child (Johnson)
Joe Burnett and his wife   Two young girls

Oak Grove Cemetery

Location: Coordinates 07782040. From S.R.16 take Rifle Range Road north for 2,800 meters. Turn right onto an unimproved dirt road and travel east for 1,050 meters. Turn left at the "T" intersection and travel northwest for 150 meters to cemetery gate.

Size: 80 by 40 meters.

Grave sites: 25

Names on the markers:

Infant son of Mr. and Mrs. O.E. O'Lemons

Missouri Everett	Louvinia Prevatt
Joe Starling	Dorothy Lee Guthrie
Minnie Lee Guthrie	Mable Ellen Guthrie
Anna May Guthrie	Abe Tarling
Addie Tarling	Burtice Boree
Lottie Boree	Jim Starling
Joseph H. Starling	Mary E. Starling
Mrs. Luverma McCormick	
Sharon McCormick	
Arcansas Woods	Rev. J.W. Wood
Matton (or Milton)	Catherine S. Riggs
P.M. Riggs	Gullford Austin
Deese	Wes

BLUE POND CEMETERY

Location: Coordinates 00100505. Starting from the boat ramp at Blue Pond, take the tank trail which runs southeast. Approximately 200 meters down the trail, take the unmarked trail that branches off to the right at a thirty-five degree angle. Follow that trail until it ends. The cemetery will be on the left.

Size: 25 by 30 meters

Grave sites: 6

Names on the markers:

Louisa Coleman	Moses Coleman
Martha Johnson	The Yates Family
M.D.	L.C.

LEE CEMETERY

Location: Coordinates 01750335. Starting from the Lowry Lake boat ramp, travel northeast along the dirt road and cross the creek that runs into the northwest corner of Lowry Lake. Continue trveling uphill and bear to the left on a dirt road. Follow that road for approximately 300 meters until the cemetery is reached. The cemetery sits on the left side of the road near the top of the ridge.

Size: 25 by 30 meters.

Grave sites: 8

Names on the markers:

SWL	Benjamin C. Lee
Sidney W. Lee	Isaac Jarrett
James F. Stewart	N. Wallace Hewes
"Mother" Griffis	Manning Griffis

CONWAY CEMETERY

Location: Coordinates 08401715. Travel east on S.R. 16 from the intersection of Routes 215 and 16 for 2,550 meters. Just before crossing Bull Creek turn left into a narrow trail. The trail is wide enough for a small four-wheel drive vehicle and is partly submerged. Travel north on the trail for 150 meters. The cemetery is approximately 150 meters uphill on a magnetic azimuth of 290 degrees.

Size: 20 by 20 meters.

Grave sites: 3

Names on the markers:

Charles Conway   Ellis Conway   C.C.

PRISONER OF WAR CEMETERY

Location: Coordinates 08021295. From the paved road intersection at 07851305, travel southeast on broken paved road to the first left turn. Turn left and travel northeast for 25 meters to the first right turn. Turn right and follow the dirt road southeast through two curves. The cemetery is located 5 meters off the left side of the road just after the curve.

Size: 20 by 30 meters.

Grave sites: None. The seven prisoners interred here were moved in 1946 to the Fort Benning, Georgia, Cemetery. The old cemetery site remains with markers showing the original burial sites. Old records of the Quartermaster General show that the German Prisoners of War who were interred at Camp Blanding were CPL Franz Klose, PVT Heinrich Baumgartner, PVT Karl Behrens, PFC Vitus Erler, PFC Georg Moos, PFC Rudolph Stamicar and PFC Wendelin Sturm.

WORLD WAR II COMBAT RECORDS OF THE BLANDING DIVISIONS

Camp Blanding Museum personnel are so impressed with the combat records of the nine divisions which trained here in the 1940s that they always refer to them as the "Blanding Divisions."

Veterans of those divisions further established a close relationship with Camp Blanding by their unanimous favorable response to the opportunity to erect a monument in the Memorial Park.

What follows is a brief summary of the World War II combat record of these divisions. Casualty figures in these summaries are taken from the most recent (1984) edition of *World War II Order of Battle* by Shelby E. Stanton. The figures are subject to question by historians who have done additional research on original records.

1st Infantry Division

Category: Regular Army

Campaign Credits: Algeria-French Morocco, Tunisia, Sicily, Normandy, Northern France, Rhineland, Ardennes-Alsace, Central Europe.

Casualties: Killed in Action 3,616. Wounded in Action 15,208. Died of Wounds 664.

Medal of Honor Awards: 16

The 1st Infantry Division, known as "The Big Red One" because of the red numeral on the shoulder patch, was one of the first to go into combat. It went ashore in Algeria in November 1942 and fought alongside the British in a series of battles in Algeria and Tunisia, taking thousands of prisoners. The 1st lost 794 men in North Africa.

The 1st made another amphibious assault landing on Sicily in July 1943. In thirty-seven days of combat it took eighteen cities and lost 264 men.

After further training the 1st landed on bloody Omaha Beach, Normandy, on D-Day June 6, 1944. It suffered heavy casualties but fought its way inland while destroying a whole German division. In July the division broke through out of Normandy, trapped 30,000 Germans near Coutances, then moved 300 miles in a week to take Soissons. The division continued fighting to Aachen, Hurtgen Forest, the Ardennes and then swept deep into Germany.

29TH INFANTRY DIVISION

Category: National Guard

Campaign Credits: Normandy, Northern France, Rhineland, Central Europe.

Casualties: Killed in Action 3,887. Wounded in Action 15,541. Died of Wounds 899.

Medal of Honor Awards: 2

The first combat experience of the 29th was to spearhead, along with the 1st Division, the Omaha Beach, Normandy, landing on D-Day, June 6, 1944. It suffered heavy casualties from heavy German fire on the beaches but overcame the odds by fighting inland off the beaches with many acts of heroism.

From Omaha Beach the 29th moved on to Isigny, St. Lo, Vire and Brest. From there the division moved on the Roer River, attacked northeast of Aachen and took a series of cities. The next objective for the 29th was the Rhine. The division captured 48 more occupied towns, then marched victoriously into Munchen-Gladbach.

By war's end, the 29th had joined with the Russians at the Elbe deep in Germany.

30TH INFANTRY DIVISION
  Category: National Guard
  Campaign Credits: Normandy, Northern France, Ardennes-Alsace,Rhineland, Central Europe.
  Casualties: Killed in Action 3,003. Wounded in Action 13,376. Died of Wounds 513.
  Medal of Honor Awards: 6

The 30th Division began its fighting in Normandy June 15, 1944, nine days after D-Day and quickly made up for the lost time. The division crossed the Vire River headed for St. Lo and soon spearheaded the breakthrough out of the hedgerows onto the plains of central France, advancing to Mortain to relieve the 1st Division. An attack by four German armored divisions hit the area of the 30th in an effort to split the American forces and drive to the sea. The 30th and its adjacent units stood firm with many acts of heroism in the face of heavy casualties. This was known as the Battle of Mortain and was stated by the German High Command to be the most important battle leading to eventual defeat of the German Army.

The 30th assisted in closing the Falaise Gap, then racing eastward, crossed the Seine and moved on to become the first American division to enter Belgium on Sept. 2, 1944, and Holland on Sept 12, capturing the fortress of Eben Emael in Belgium and liberating Maastricht in Holland. After this the division assaulted the Siegfried Line, broke through the massive fortifications and made contact with the 1st Division. The two divisions then encircled Aachen, which capitulated Oct 21, 1944.

When the Battle of the Bulge began on Dec 16, the 30th went to the Malmedy-Stavelot sector of the Ardennes and joined the fighting there. When the counterattack was stopped, the 30th returned to the Roer River, making a major assault and breakthrough, then raced for the Rhine and helped bottle up thousands of enemy soldiers in the Ruhr pocket. When the war ended in Europe, the 30th was in the area of Magdeburg. The division became part of the Army of Occupation until August 1945, returned to the United States and was deactivated in November 1945. The 30th gained the nickname of the "Workhorse of the Western Front."

31st Infantry Division
Category: National Guard
Campaign Credits: New Guinea, Southern Philippines
Casualties: Killed in Action 340. Wounded in Action 1,392. Died of Wounds 74.
Medal of Honor Awards: 1

The 31st "Dixie Division" had about as many northerners as southerners when it went into battle. After brief training in the bush of Oro Bay, New Guinea, the regiments of the 31st went into combat. One combat team went to Aitape, the other two to Wakde-Sarmi. The action at Aitape was bloody fighting along the Driniumor River where the 124th Infantry killed more than 3,000 enemy. Fighting was lighter at Wakde-Sarmi but the 155th and 167th regiments accounted for more than 1,000 enemy.

On September 15 the 31st hit the beaches of the Dutch island of Morotai, less than 350 miles from the Philippines. By noon of D-Day the division seized Pitoe Airdrome. Morotai cut off 20,000 Japanese troops. The 31st then maintained a perimeter defense for the 30th Air Force with its men living on outposts for weeks at a time.

On April 22, 1945, the 31st, along with the 24th Division, landed on the island of Mindanao in the southern Philippines. Bloody fighting ensued at the Maramag Airstrip where the Americans suffered heavy casualties but routed the enemy after six days of heavy fighting. The division continued north against diminishing opposition.

36TH INFANTRY DIVISION

Category: National Guard

Campaign Credits: Naples-Foggia, Anzio, Rome-Arno, Southern France, Rhineland, Ardennes-Alsace, Central Europe.

Casualties: Killed in Action 3,131. Wounded in Action 13,191. Died of Wounds 506.

Medal of Honor Awards: 14

The 36th Division experienced its first combat when it went ashore at Salerno in September 1943 after training in North Africa. It suffered heavy casualties on the beachhead. The 36th forced its way inland and secured the area from Agropoli to Alatavilla. It was here that Corporal Charles E. Kelly displayed such heroic actions that he got the nickname "Commando" and was awarded the Medal of Honor.

After the battle for Cassino and a few weeks of rest, the 36th joined the beachhead forces at Anzio and helped pave the way for the fall of Rome.

The division made another landing in southern France in August 1944, took many objectives and moved 300 miles to reach the foothills of the Vosges mountains facing the Moselle River. They established a bridgehead, then continued to drive ahead. The 36th experienced 132 consecutive days of combat smashing across the Rhine and deep into the heart of Germany.

43RD INFANTRY DIVISION
    Category: National Guard
    Campaign Credits: Guadalcanal, Northern Solomons, New Guinea, Luzon.
    Casualties: Killed in Action 1,128. Wounded in Action 4,887. Died of Wounds 278.
    Medal of Honor Awards: 2

The 43rd Division reached New Zealand in October 1942 when it appeared likely the Japanese might invade that country. In February 1943 it helped mopping-up operations on Guadalcanal. It then occupied the Russell Islands without opposition and took Vangunu and Rendova against minor resistance. It met heavy resistance and many Japanese tricks on New Georgia in one of the roughest battles of the early war in the Pacific. The 43rd, with elements of the 37th Division, captured the vital Munda Airfield in August 1943.

The next combat for the 43rd was Northern New Guinea where the division landed at Aitape and helped stop large elements of Japanese forces trying to cross the Driniumor River.

The 43rd Division was part of the initial invasion of Luzon on January 9, 1945 at Lingayen Gulf. The division sustained extremely heavy casualties for the next month while fighting to take a series of hills held by tenacious Japanese troops. The division fought in further heavy actions in southwestern Luzon, east-central Luzon and the area around Manila. The 43rd captured the Ipo Dam which supplied water for the city of Manila.

63RD INFANTRY DIVISION
    Category: New division, Army Reserve, activated at Camp Blanding
    Campaign Credits: Rhineland, Central Europe.
    Casualties: Killed in Action 861. Wounded in Action 3,326. Died of Wounds 113. [NOTE: Recent original research by William J. Scott, historian of this division has found additional

totals. The division monument at Camp Blanding shows total casualties 8,019]

Medal of Honor Awards: 2

Activated at Camp Blanding in June 1943, the 63rd Division joined the combat action in Europe in December 1944 protecting the eastern flank of the Seventh Army along the Rhine River. The following month the regiments of the 63rd were fighting in separate actions, the 253rd and 255th in Alsace and the 254th in a series of major battles in the Colmar pocket.

In February 1945 the division re-assembled, crossed the Saar River and led the Seventh Army back onto German soil and penetrated the lower Siegfried Line. In April the 63rd destroyed the German Seventeenth SS Division, forced the enemy into retreat, then pursued them through Wurttemberg and Bavaria across the Danube River to Landsberg at the edge of the Bavarian Alps.

66TH INFANTRY DIVISION

Cagegory: New division

Campaign Credits: Northern France

Casualties: Killed in Action 795. Wounded in Action 636. Died of Wounds 5.

Medal of Honor Awards: 0

The 66th "Black Panther" Division reached England in early December, 1944 and began crossing the English Channel to Cherbourg December 24th. A German U-Boat torpedoed one of the transport ships, and fourteen officers and 748 enlisted men were lost. Nevertheless, on December 29 the division was assigned the mission of containing the 50,000 German troops in the ports of Lorient and St. Nazaire on the south coast of Brittany.

The 66th carried out this important, if not glamorous, mission and prevented these first-rate German troops from threatening the rear of the Allied lines. They also protected the local populace from the Nazis. The division was involved in many patrol clashes and repulsed a heavy attack near La Croix with heavy casualties on the Germans. The German troops surrendered to the 66th upon the termination of hostilities May 8, 1945.

79TH INFANTRY DIVISION

Category: Army Reserve, Activated for World War II June 15, 1942

Campaign Credits: Normandy, Northern France, Rhineland, Ardennes-Alsace, Central Europe.

Casualties: Killed in Action 2,476. Wounded in Action 10,971. Died of Wounds 467.

Medal of Honor Awards: 3

The 79th Division landed in Normandy on D-plus six days and entered combat on June 19, 1944 with an attack near Valognes. After helping cut off the Cotentin Peninsula, the 79th attacked up the peninsula against strong German resistance, took Fort Du Roule and entered Cherbourg where it engaged in fierce street battles.

Despite heavy casualties in hedgerow fighting, the 79th seized La Haye-du-Puits, nerve center of the German supply system in Normandy on July 8, then repulsed heavy counterattacks. Cherbourg surrendered on July 26. The 79th made a rapid move ahead to reach the Seine River August 19, established a bridgehead and captured the German Army Group Headquarters.

The 79th then engaged in a series of major battles as far north as Tournai, Belgium, Charmes, Baccarat and the forest of Parroy and across the Rhine deep into Germany.

508TH PARACHUTE INFANTRY

In the history of Camp Blanding the 508th Parachute Infantry takes its place alongside the nine "Blanding Divisions" because it was activated and took its major training at Camp

Blanding before embarking on its historic combat roles in Europe.

The 508th arrived in northern Ireland in January 1944 and was attached to the 82nd Airborne Division until January 1945. The regiment's first combat was on D-Day when it jumped into Normandy at 2:30A.M. on June 6, 1944. After thirty-three days in combat, the 508th returned to England.

Its next combat jump was into Holland on September 17, 1944, for fifty-two days of combat. It then returned to France but was sent by truck into the Battle of the Bulge, December 17, 1944, and remained in combat until February 18, 1945.

After V-E Day, the 508th moved to Frankfurt, Germany, to serve as honor guard for General Eisenhower's headquarters.

SOURCES

BOOKS

Blakey, Arch Fredric, *Parade of Memories, A History of Clay County, Florida,* Clay County Bicentennial Steering Committee, 1976.

Collins, Brig. Gen. Vivian, *Historical Annual,* National Guard of the State of Florida, 1939."

Ewing, Joseph H., *29 Let's Go! A History of the 29th Infantry Division in World War II.* Infantry Journal Press, Washington, D.C. 1948.

Hewitt, Robert L., *Work Horse of the Western Front, The Story of the 30th Infantry Division.* Infantry Journal Press, Washington, D.C. 1946

Huff, SSG Richard A., editor, *A Pictorial History of the 36th Division,* compiled by 36th Division Pictorial History Team.

Persons, Maj. Gen. John C., commander, *History of the 31st Infantry Division in the Pacific.*

Schmidt, Lewis G., *The Civil War in Florida, A Military History, Volume II*, The Battle of Olustee, published by Lewis G. Schmidt, Allentown, PA, 1989.

Wessman, Siinto S., *66—A Story of World War II*, 1946, reprinted by The Battery Press, Nashville, TN.

Zimmer, Joseph E., *The History of the 43rd Infantry Division, 1941-1945*, Army and Navy Publishing Co., Baton Route, LA, no publication date shown.

Anon., *Camp Blanding Museum and Memorial Park of the Second World War with Unit Historical Summaries*, prepared by Camp Blanding Museum and Historical Associates, Inc., undated.

Anon., *History of the 43rd Infantry Division.* Army and Navy Publishing Co., Inc., Baton Rouge, LA 1941.

Anon., *History of the 508th Parachute Infantry*, reprinted by The Battery Press, Nashville, TN, 1977.

PAMPHLETS

"IRTC Handbook, Camp Blanding, Florida," produced by Special Service, Infantry Replacement Training Center, Camp Blanding, FL.

"I Am a Doughboy," Infantry Replacement Training Center pamphlet describing individual Army jobs for which recruits were being trained. Camp Blanding, FL.

"Description and History—Camp Blanding Military Reservation," Office of The Adjutant General, St. Augustine, FL, 1976.

The Bulletin, Official Publicity Organ of the 43rd National Guard Division," published by the division at induction into federal service in 1941.

"Welcome, Soldier," Separation Center, Camp Blanding, Florida. Undated.

"Organized Reserve Corps," Memorandum for All Officers, War Department, Washington,D.C. Aug. 24, 1945.

NEWSPAPERS

Bradford County Telegraph, Starke, FL. Many issues of the period 1939-1945, the 110th anniversary edition, a series of historical articles 1991-1992, and subsequent issues reporting recent events.

Camp Blanding Report, official post newspaper, from its inception April 5, 1944 to Oct. 31, 1945.

Omaha (NE) World-Herald, May 29, 1945, article "'Pick's Pike' Is Miracle Highway Job."

Blanding Bugle, issues published for Camp Blanding Training Site 1990-1996 by *Bradford County Telegraph*.

Orlando Sentinel, issues of October 12-15, 1986, articles about World War II prisoners of war in Florida by Bill Bond.

OTHER PUBLICATIONS

Reports of The Adjutant General of Florida, biennial for the years 1939-1940 through 1967—1968, annual for the years 1969 through 1995. Office of The Adjutant General, St. Augustine, FL.

Annual Reports of the Commander, Camp Blanding Station Hospital, to The Surgeon General of the Army, 1941—1943.

The Military Engineer, November 1944, article "Along the Ledo Road" by John R. McDowell.

InfoTrac, Smithsonian, June 1995, "By Convention, the Enemy Within Never Did Without" by Jack Fincher.

Florida Historical Quarterly, 1979 date uncertain, article "With the Wehrmacht in Florida: The German POW Facility at Camp Blanding, 1942—1946," by Robert D. Billinger, Jr.

Florida Highways magazine, Florida State Road Department, Oct. 1943.

C of C Chronicle, Gainesville Chamber of Commerce, January 1944.

UNPUBLISHED PAPERS

Correspondence files of The Adjutant General of Florida, 1939—1943.

"The Genesis of Camp Blanding," by Brig Gen Ralph W. Cooper, Jr., undated.

Frisbie, Maj Sayer L. IV, "Camp Blanding, Florida, in War and Peace," for Subcourse 85/7, United States Army Command and General Staff College, Fort Leavenworth, KS. 1979.

"Camp Blanding Historic Preservation Plan and Memorandum of Agreement," Department of the Army, Mobile District, Corps of Engineers, Mobile, AL June 28, 1988.

Regimental History, 45th Engineer Regiment (GS), two copies, January 1, 1942 to December 31, 1942 and January 1, 1943 to December 31, 1943.

"Survey of Cemeteries Located on the Camp Blanding Training Site," prepared by Captain Michael A. O'Brien, FLARNG, 21 September 1987.

"Analysis of Camp Blanding, Florida," Post War Utilization Studies by War Department Office of the Chief of Engineers, September 1945..

"History of Land Acquisition for Camp Blanding," Board of County Commissioners, Clay County, letter with enclosures by William D. Moore, county attorney, May 3, 1984.

"Camp Blanding Training Site Facilities Master Plan," Section 3, History, undated.

"Recollections of Camp Blanding During World War II," provided to the author by Leon S. Theil, Captain, AUS-Ret., Sept 4, 1995.

"Record of Visit to Camp," report of visit to Camp Blanding Prisoner of War Camp 26—29 December 1943 by Captain Edward C. Shannahan.

OTHER MATERIALS

Recollections of Camp Blanding 1942—1946, audio tape supplied to the author by Julian K. Wood, October 1995.

Excerpts from letters sent home from Camp Blanding 1945—1946 by Richard W. Stark, supplied by him to Camp Blanding Museum.

Interviews and Correspondence

Salvatore Bazzano, Yonkers, NY
Mrs. Helen Black, Kansas City, MO
Robert B. Bradley, Gettysburg, PA
Fred D. Brenner, Studio City, CA
Kris Dalane, Charlotte, NC
Dr. Samuel Day, Jacksonville, FL
Sidney Eichen, Hollywood, FL
William Faust, St. Augustine Shores, FL
Rodney P. Hall, Starke, FL
James F. Hammond, Corry, PA
Harry M. Hatcher, Starke, FL
Karen Jenks, Redondo Beach, CA
Gabriel Lazar, Satellite Beach, FL
George Lovell, Starke, FL
James V. Maguire, Wakefield, MA
Eugene Maurey, Chicago, IL
Walter M. Morawski, Pittsfield, MA
Frank E. Nipper, Jacksonville, FL
Robert M. Phillips, Middleburg, FL
William A. Pillsbury, Lutherville, MD
Thomas L. Raney, Fairfax Station, VA
William J. Scott, Sycamore, IL
William G. Smith Sr., Madison, OH
Henry M. Stairs, Ligonier, PA
Donald D. Taylor, Watertown, CT

Earl A. Taylor, Dennisport, MA
Leon S. Theil, Marco Island, FL
Frank W. Towers, Brooker, FL
Frank R. Vogel, Ft. Myers, FL
Sydney Williams, Starke, FL
Robert L. Wilson, Miami, FL
Julian K. Wood, Bagdad, KY
Dr. Mary Zellner, Green Cove Springs, FL

About The Author

Florida writer Major General W. Stanford Smith (Ret.) is a native of Georgia who began his successful military career when he was commissioned from ROTC at the University of Georgia in 1941. Serving in many assignments from commandant of an Army Reserve school to an appointment by President Johnson to election observer team for national elections in South Vietnam in 1967, General Smith has shown to the public the attributes of an American soldier. He received the Defense Distinguished Service Medal in 1979 after retiring from his position of Executive Officer of Reserve Forces Policy Board, office of the Secretary of Defense.

He is author of *The Cannoneers*, a book based on his commander experience during World War II. He is a founding member and first vice-president, as well as past president of Camp Blanding Museum and Historical Association. Additionally, he served as chairman of the dedication planning committee for the Camp Blanding Museum and Memorial Park. He dedicates this work to the citizen soldiers who faithfully served at Camp Blanding, then and now.